Pilgrimage

Pilgrimage

A Handbook on Christian Growth

Richard Peace

Foreword by Lyman Coleman

BAKER BOOK HOUSE
Grand Rapids, Michigan 49506

To Louise Pickins
"Akka"
True Pilgrim

Acknowledgments

Many people have contributed to this book, and I am grateful for their input. I first presented the core ideas of PILGRIMAGE in the form of an adult Sunday School class at Newton Presbyterian Church in Newton, Massachusetts, and profited from the interchange that took place then. I have appreciated, too, working with Acton House in this venture. George Baskin provided needed encouragement right from the beginning when PILGRIMAGE was nothing more than an outline and a few ideas; and Nancy Bundy has undertaken the editorial work with a vigor and an attention to detail that I have greatly valued.

Winki Bliss not only typed (and re-typed) the whole manuscript—a formidable job given my sub-standard penmanship—but also interacted usefully with its ideas. My wife, Judy, was, as usual, the source of many ideas. Her special perceptions and her constant insistence upon facing up to the way things really are (as against how we would like them to be) have added vital dimensions to PILGRIMAGE.

Special thanks must go to David Nelson, my good friend and collaborator on many a project. David spent numerous hours working through the manuscript in detail—helping to pare away the superfluities and to re-order the text so it flowed more smoothly. His help, needless to say, has been invaluable.

I also want to add a word of thanks to Lyman Coleman. I greatly appreciated his willingness to take time from his incredibly busy schedule to work through PILGRIMAGE in detail and then to write the Foreword. His kind words have been very affirming for me.

Grateful acknowledgment is made to the following publishers for permission to reprint copyright material:

Dialogue House for an excerpt from *At a Journal Workshop*, by Ira Progoff, © 1975.

Foreword

"You ought to read this book," my wife suggested in her own subtle, non-direct way.

"I intend to," I replied, "I am going to write the foreword to it."

"I mean—you ought to read this for *yourself*," she came back.

I had a sneaking suspicion what my wife was alluding to. For a couple of years now, I have been in a "holding pattern" in my own spiritual pilgrimage, waiting for the cloud cover to disappear so that I could understand more clearly what God is trying to say to me.

Call it emotional fatigue, the "mid-life crisis," or just my own neurotic temperament, I sometimes feel that I have "peaked out" in my pilgrimage. I suppose the day-to-day plodding for nearly twenty-five years with a Vince Lombardi "give it all you've got" mentality has had its toll on me. More often than not, I find myself with Elijah under the gourd tree.

Anyway, this is where I was coming from when I picked up this manuscript. I needed a little insight into the causes for "peaking out" spiritually, from a fellow pilgrim that I could respect. And I was not disappointed in what I found.

Dick grabbed me right away with the case history about his own "early days" as a Christian warrior, back in the "good ole days" when everything was black and white. Having come from a similar background, I found myself smiling (and cringing) at many of the anecdotes. I didn't get the impression that Dick was trying to make fun of his heritage, but rather to help those of us who have come from a similar heritage to integrate the best of our past with contemporary philosophical, theological and psychological understanding.

I guess the thing I appreciate most about Dick Peace is his willingness to deal with the questions that might be considered unsafe for a thorough going evangelical scholar, and to use his own struggles as Exhibit A. His honesty and gentle prodding gave me a chance to surface some of my own struggles, without harboring a sense of guilt for feeling as I do.

I see this book helping a lot of us to take a second look at where we are right now in our pilgrimage, and to move on. His practical advice for working through the road-blocks, and the homework assignments at the end of each chapter are added encouragements to keep moving.

As I reached the end of the book, I found myself breathing a sigh of relief. Someone had helped me tell my own story. It was O.K. to be where I am right now, so long as I don't stop now. I owe a debt of gratitude to my friend, Dick Peace, for his courage and insight in writing this book. And I heartily recommend it to all foot-sore pilgrims.

LYMAN COLEMAN

Contents

Acknowledgments vi
Foreword ix
Introduction 1
 Inter Action: Preparing for Growth 3

Part I: Pilgrimage: The Key to Wholeness 5
Chapter One: The Settler 6
 Inter Action: The Pilgrim/Settler Quiz 12
Chapter Two: The Pilgrim 16
 Inter Action: Pilgrim Images 16
     Strangers and Pilgrims: A Study
     of Hebrews 11:13-16 26
Chapter Three: The Psychology of Growth 30
 Inter Action: The New Psychology 35

Part II: The Geography of Pilgrimage 37
Chapter Four: Charting Our Pilgrimage 38
 Inter Action: Charting 45
Chapter Five: Quest 48
 Inter Action: Seeking Truth 59
Chapter Six: Commitment 64
 Inter Action: Commitments 70
Chapter Seven: Encounter 73
 Inter Action: Meeting Jesus 81
Chapter Eight: Integration 84
 Inter Action: Repentance/Faith Images 84
     Repenting 94

Part III: Blockages to Growth   99
   Chapter Nine: "Fighting Without": External Impediments
                to Christian Growth   100
      Inter Action: Groups   110
   Chapter Ten: "Fear Within": Internal Obstacles to Growth   112
      Inter Action: Fighting Fears and Finding Motivation   124

Part IV: Resources for Growth   129
   Chapter Eleven: External Resources   131
      Inter Action: Using Resources   140
   Chapter Twelve: Inner Resources   142
      Inter Action: Inner Visions   153
   Chapter Thirteen: The Dynamics of Change   155
      Inter Action: Plotting Personal Change   158
   Pilgrimage Bibliography   160
   Notes   162

Introduction

As a teen-ager, growing up in an evangelical church in Detroit, I discovered that there existed a highly prized attribute called "the zeal of a new Christian." To be pointed out as possessing this "zeal" was a high mark of approval. This "zeal," I came to find out, was the enthusiastic way in which new Christians threw themselves into the life of the church. They attended every meeting with relish. They happily did any job given to them. They even longed for jobs! They could not get enough teaching. And they actually took notes during sermons.

At the time, being a new Christian myself and exhibiting all the characteristics of this very zeal, I was a bit puzzled by the wistful way in which this was spoken about by older church members. I now understand the wistfulness.

Zeal is not a quality which characterizes the lives of many Christians. There comes a point, it seems, when meetings become routine and we find excuses for staying home to watch T.V.; when we groan inwardly as we are asked to join yet another committee; when we begin Sunday School in the fall with high hopes only to find in a month or two that we already know most of what is being taught. As for sermons, well, perhaps there will be a new anecdote that can jolt us into full attention for a few moments.

This movement from zeal to complacency has long puzzled me—and not just in an academic way. As I look back on my own Christian experience, I remember — wistfully — the sheer excitement and fun of the Bible Studies we had on Sunday evenings in the High School lounge. I remember the enthusiasm with which we passed out tracts at a local shopping mall, and the anticipation we shared as we set up folding chairs for an outdoor evangelistic meeting in the slums of Detroit. I recall the unquestioning faith with which we prayed for Africa each afternoon after classes finished at Seminary. But I also remember, in more recent years,

1

the lack of enthusiasm for attending yet another Sunday morning service and the dread of forthcoming committee meetings. I know all about the fulfillment of church commitments out of a sense of responsibility and nothing more.

Is this the norm? Does one begin with dedication and enthusiasm and then inexorably lose that zeal, ending up with either complacent membership or, even worse, disillusionment and bitterness? That this happens within the church is without question. That it has to happen is another story.

How then can we avoid this numbing complacency? The answer to this question is not, of course, an easy one. The attempt to answer it comprises this book.

In the pages which follow, I will seek to analyze the dynamics of Christian growth; the obstacles which inhibit growth; and the resources, both external and internal, that promote growth. In this discussion I will refer frequently to a pair of related images: that of the pilgrim and that of the settler. I use these images because I see in the pilgrim the model for what our Christian life is intended to be; whereas in the settler one has a picture of how we are tempted to pattern our life in order to avoid further growth.[1] The book is also the story of various pilgrimages, often my own, that illustrate the ideas under discussion. However, it is not just an extended essay on Christian growth. It also seeks to be an *aid* to personal growth in and of itself. Each chapter contains text in which the main points are set out, but the text is followed by a section entitled "Inter Action," in which the reader is invited to undertake various exercises that are designed to help him come to grips in a personal, experiential way with the concepts that have just been presented. It is strongly recommended that the exercises be undertaken. Without them, *Pilgrimage* remains just another book, interesting (it's hoped), but remote from the real business of growing and changing.

▶ Inter Action

Preparing for Growth

I. A Notebook on Growth

At the end of each chapter (and occasionally at the beginning) is the "Inter Action" section related to the ideas of that chapter. I would suggest that you begin work on the related exercise as soon as you finish each chapter, while the ideas are fresh in your mind.

These exercises generally ask for a written response. Where it seemed appropriate to add clarification, I have given abbreviated examples, often out of my own experience. I would suggest that you obtain a looseleaf notebook in which to do the work that is asked for. This notebook will serve as a storage place for all the exercises and as a convenient place in which to make notes on what you read, or to record various thoughts that come to mind as you work through *Pilgrimage*. These personal insights often provide keys to understanding where we are as people and the way we are meant to go.

Now that you have your notebook in hand, and before you go on to Chapter One, do the following exercise.

II. Images of Growth: An Exercise in Memory

A. Think back over your past experience. Can you identify any individuals who are examples to you of Christians who always seem to be growing? List their names.

(Example: E. Stanley Jones)

B. Now think about these individuals, one at a time. Picture them in your mind. What is it about them, in terms of Christian growth, that attracted your attention?

(Example: —he always seemed to have fresh insights
—radiated an inner vitality and energy
—didn't settle down but constantly gave out
—seemed to be in touch in a vital way with the Living God)

C. From what you know about these people, what elements in their lives might account for their growth?

(Example: —his time each day spent alone in prayer and meditation
              —his openness to new input and willingness
                to think about the new thing until he understood it
              —wheat germ and push-ups)

D. In terms of your own life, what is it about the life and experience
of these various people that is relevant to you now?

III. Bibliography

Dedication and Leadership: Learning from the Communists, by Douglas Hyde (Notre Dame, Indiana: Notre Dame Press, 1966) is a very
readable and fascinating study which looks at *why* it is that Communism
has been able to motivate its followers to "change the world." This book
also deals with the whole question of the "loss of zeal," albeit from a
totally different point of view. Douglas Hyde was a long-time Communist
who became a Christian and has extracted valuable lessons for the
church from his experience with the Communist Party.

Part I
Pilgrimage:
The Key to Wholeness

The wind is old and still at play
While I must hurry upon my way
For I am running to Paradise

    —William Butler Yeats

1 The Settler

It was good to be back home. Despite how often I had said: "Detroit—it's a nice place to be *from*," still this had been my home for the first twenty years of my life and it was filled with rich memories. I was especially looking forward to visiting the church where I had been a member for so long. I had joined this particular church as a teenager and it was there that my early growth as a Christian had taken place.

As I drove to church Sunday morning with my parents, I remembered how much fun it had been during my teen-age years. Life then had been an unending round of church activities: Bible studies, skating parties, singspirations, testimonies, Sunday School, and fellowship—especially fellowship. At the church I was part of a group and I was accepted and loved. Looking back now it was easy to see why all of this had provided the shape and focus for my life as I went away to college and then seminary and finally to the mission field. The experiences had all been so positive.

As we pulled into the parking lot, it was evident that the church had expanded since I was last in Detroit. A whole new wing had been added. It had grown in membership, too, I later found out. Once in the door, it was an unending round of handshakes, back-pats, and smiles until the morning service began. I had many friends there.

After the service, several friends related what had happened at the church during the past few years while they gave me a grand tour of the building. Despite the new building, it was all very familiar. In fact, I began to realize that except for the physical changes, the church seemed exactly the same as it had been when I left ten years previously. Certainly the service that morning had been identical to many I had sat through in years gone by. The programs appeared to be the same. The people were talking about the same subjects. The aspirations and plans had not changed.

It struck me like a thunderbolt. It was the same. Nothing had really changed. No one had grown very much. By and large, the people in the congregation were virtually all at the same place in their spiritual pilgrimage that they had been ten years previously.

What had been an impression was confirmed in the days that followed as I spent time with my friends from the church. As I listened, I kept hearing echoes from the past. The activities planned for the youth group were the activities we had experienced—but the kids of the 70's were so different than we had been in the 50's. The missionary conference was run along the same lines as it had always been, complete with the same appeal—even though the nature and needs of the mission field had undergone radical change—as had the opportunities for mission service.

I suppose the most telling experience came when I tried to share where I was in my Christian growth—how, for example, my understanding of Christian social responsibility had grown as a result of our years in Africa living face to face with poverty; how I had come to see while living in South Africa that a conversion experience by itself did not automatically change the way a White related to a Black, etc. There was not much enthusiasm for conversation about these things. In fact, some friends seemed downright uncomfortable about what I had been learning.

I was sad when I left Detroit. I felt no less love for all my friends at the church, but I was sad that so many of them seemed to be in a box—a warm, comfortable and secure box to be sure, but still a box, and the net result was that their growth as Christians had been stifled. They had become settlers, when they should have been pilgrims.

Yet, I thought, if the people there had been asked in a quiz one Sunday: "Is a Christian meant to be a pilgrim or a settler?", since it is a biblically literate congregation, most would probably have replied correctly, "A pilgrim." And then, if pressed as to whether they themselves were living the life of a pilgrim, I suspect again that most would have affirmed that, "Yes," they were.

It is not easy to see ourselves and our life-style clearly, especially if there is a disjunction between what we know we are supposed to be and what we really are. But growth begins by discovering where we really are. So I think it is important that we begin by sketching out just what it means to be a settler and then (in the next chapter) what it means to be a pilgrim, so that each of us will have a basis on which to judge the way we are really living. Are we actually pilgrims or really just settlers? How can I tell whether my basic orientation to life is that of a pilgrim or that of a settler? What is a settler after all? What does his life-style look like? What attitudes characterize him?

The most important characteristic of a settler is that he has stopped moving; or at least he has limited his movements of growth to a fairly well-defined sphere. In other words, he has found a "position," claimed it as his own, and settled down to live within its confines.

I don't think most of us intend to become settlers. It is just that at some point we find ourselves in a really congenial atmosphere. We feel comfortable there. We fit. We are accepted. We share the group's beliefs, tastes, and ways of looking at the world. So, we stop. Sure, we may not be learning much that is new nor having any particularly meaningful spiritual experience . . . but by and large, we are content.

And it's easy to understand *why* we stop. There are many advantages to the life of a settler over that of a pilgrim. It's cold and dangerous out there in the world as a pilgrim. There is no telling who you might meet and how they might influence you. The world is a dangerous environment filled with wrong, even Satanic ideas, that do have power in and of themselves. Whereas in a secure environment, with well-defined and well-defended boundaries, there is a sort of peace.

Boundaries are very important for the settler. They are the thing that gives shape and definition to his existence. They also define for him the people with whom he can safely associate, the ideas he can espouse, and the activities he can enjoy.

There are at least two different kinds of boundaries. First of all, there are idea-related boundaries. Certain groups are characterized by a set of shared beliefs. In Christian terms, these shared ideas are often theological in nature. To be a member of that particular group you are asked to affirm certain doctrines and to deny others which are deemed aberrant.

Secondly, there are attitudinal boundaries. People in this group all share pretty much the same feelings about certain issues, be they political, racial, economic or ecclesiastical. Take, for example, attitudes toward worship. Certain churches are characterized not so much by their doctrinal stance (which might be quite loose) as they are by the way their worship service is conducted. Members of that congregation will have quite definite ideas as to the order of worship, the type of hymns and prayers used, and what constitutes an acceptable sermon. Heaven help anyone who tries to introduce new elements.

I have been talking as if boundaries were developed exclusively by local churches. This is, of course, not the case. The particular boundaries that are meaningful may be those that define a denomination; characterize a para-church group like Campus Crusade for Christ or Faith at Work; or are shared by a theological grouping like "evangelicals" or "charismatics." We may even have set up our own private boundaries.

Sometimes these boundaries are very comprehensive, touching upon vast spheres of our life. Thinking back to my experience in Detroit again, I realize now just how all-embracing our boundaries were. They governed who our friends were, how we spent our time, the type of job we should hold, where we went to college, what we read, who we considered a "real Christian," and what activities were permissible. I recall that prior to joining the church I had a wide range of friends, but afterwards my real friends gradually narrowed down to those teen-agers who belonged to the few churches in the city which were considered doctrinally sound. Furthermore, my activities became more and more limited to church-related events. When I began playing church baseball and basketball, even my sports interests became church-oriented. The books I read were published by a few Christian presses. The music I listened to was recorded by Christian artists. The speakers and teachers I paid heed to all held "approved" doctrinal commitments.

The logical outcome of this sort of thinking is the development of a Christian sub-culture which seeks to isolate its people from all but minimal contact with the non-Christian world around it. That such a sub-culture existed in Detroit was made abundantly clear to me when a group of enterprising Christian businessmen set up a Christian Night Club. A secular nightclub was purchased, the bar torn out, Christian entertainment secured (*e.g.,* Gospel Trios), and the prices jacked up (to cover the loss of bar receipts). Now even your night-life could be Christian!

The problem with boundaries is that they artificially limit growth. They do this by virtue of monitoring the input that group members receive. Speakers and teachers are chosen because they share the same boundaries. Certain magazines and books are approved and circulated while others are anathematized. The same doctrines are emphasized over and over again, while others are mentioned only to be condemned. Fellowship is limited, by and large to people of like mind. There is, in other words, little unauthorized input that might lead a person to conclusions different from those shared by the group.

This screening of input can be very intense. At a Brethren Assembly which I attended sporadically during college I remember hearing of an itinerant speaker who was quizzed by the elders of another assembly in the area as to his orthodoxy and hence his right to address that particular assembly. He answered correctly all the usual doctrinal questions but still a few of the elders were uneasy. So they probed some more, now getting down to fine points of doctrine. Their persistence paid off when it finally came out that his daughter attended Emmaus Bible College, a Brethren institution, but one not accepted by that particular assembly. The man was not allowed to address the assembly that Sunday.

Boundaries are also problematic in that they can lead to a shared attitude of mistrust toward those outside the group. This attitude is often accompanied by a confidence that somehow your particular group has superior insights or ways of doing things than other groups. This serves to further intensify the individual's commitment to the group with the result that even if he is exposed to the views of others, he pays little attention to them.

Another problem with boundaries is their effect upon evangelism. It seems to be true that those groups with really rigid boundaries, particularly of an attitudinal nature, are fairly circumspect about evangelism. They do want people to discover the reality of Jesus, but they also tend to demand conformity to their whole life-style as a pre-condition to church membership. Their evangelism therefore, is often characterized by concern at a distance. Outsiders are invited into the church environment and told about Jesus, rather than church members going out into the world to be witnesses for Christ. The reason for this is clear. Outsiders just might upset the safe boundaries of the group.

I recall one particular evening at our young people's group in Detroit. The theme was evangelism and we planned to spend the evening practicing "soul winning." However, that night four or five new kids showed up for the youth group. They came with a girl whose parents were church members, although she herself had never really gotten involved in the church. We always wondered if she really was a Christian. But there she was with her friends, and no one was quite sure what to do with all of them. Nevertheless, the meeting proceeded as planned. There was little interaction, however, between the youth group and the visitors. Needless to say, the new kids never returned. The next week, however, we continued our training in evangelism.

Given the importance of boundaries to the settler, it is not surprising that a great deal of time and energy is devoted to the process of defining and defending boundaries. In fact, it seems that Christian growth for certain people comes to be understood as the process of learning more and more about doctrinal minutiae in order to know with increasing precision the exact demarcation of the group's boundaries and hence to have a clearer idea of who belongs and who does not. I can recall the vigor with which we studied and debated points of doctrine, the horror with which we greeted doctrinal deviation, and the arrogance with which we assumed that we were right and all others wrong.

The problem is that the boundaries form an artificial barrier to growth. They constantly say: "This far and no further." So that eventually a sterility enters one's life. You have learned pretty much all there is to be learned given the boundaries. So one simply grows more and more rigid in the holding of these "truths," or becomes preoccupied with matters of secondary importance. I know more than one person who can recite in great detail the meaning of all the symbols in the book of Revelation while simultaneously failing to understand on any but an elementary level the significance of Jesus' "greatest commandment."

One further word must be added to this discussion of boundaries. The real problem is not with boundaries themselves. In fact, no group can exist without boundaries, which are nothing more than its distinguishing characteristics. The problem comes when a person *limits himself* to these boundaries; when they are allowed to define for him the extent of his inquiry into God's truth, the type of people with whom he can associate, and the extent to which he can grow as a Christian. In other words, the problem comes when he allows the boundaries to define who he is rather than using them as the basis for knowing and experiencing truth. It is not the fact of boundaries that is the problem, but our attitude toward them.

So I am *not* saying that churches are wrong, doctrine is a hindrance, orthodoxy is unimportant, or even that to have a particular taste in worship is bad. In fact, it is quite clear that we all need to be part of a group. Fellowship is essential to Christian growth. Doctrine, too, is vital. Christianity is a confessional faith. It is all about God's action in history. Jesus did come as a man, lived, died for our sins; and actually rose again from the dead. These are the very foundations upon which our growth as Christians is based—and it is important that we know clearly what we believe, especially in the face of the growing secularity of our society. The problem arises when we believe our understanding of God's truth to be complete and refuse to go any further in exploring the vastness and the subtlety of His creation.

So to know whether we are living like a pilgrim or like a settler we have to take a long, hard look at our attitude toward the boundaries that encompass our lives. Do we use these structures as an excuse for not growing, or as the firm foundation from which we move deeper in our faith? Do we limit our perceptions to the confines of these boundaries, or do we use the definitions and perspectives as a means of getting a handle on differing viewpoints? Do we actively seek out data that will either explain in new depth ideas we hold or expose us to new possibilities? Is our group a temporary stopping point in an on-going pilgrimage or the end of the journey? Do the boundaries show us what we have already assimilated or tell us that we can go only so far and no further?

What about troubling areas in our life? Do we actively seek help and advice or just deny the problem or even run away from it? Have we located the "growing edge" in our experience—that point where God is trying to teach us? Or are we content to be who we are, believing what we believe with what understanding we have, living the way we live, avoiding people who are different from us?

A settler is an individual who, for one reason or another, has accepted a set of boundaries for his life which define and thus limit the nature and extent of his Christian growth. To be sure, there is some change, but it is always within fairly strict confines. Such growth is little more than pushing around the furniture of one's life from one spot to another. The dimensions of the room stay the same and the pieces of furniture remain constant. It's just that occasionally a few neglected items off in one corner get dusted off or dry cleaned. (Perhaps a visiting speaker reminds us of some doctrine we have always believed but have neglected lately.) Or, perhaps new arrangements of the furniture are tried out. But by and large, there is never any radical home improvement. Walls are never knocked out to expand the size of the place. New, large-size windows which let in lots of light just don't get put in. And heaven help anyone who suggests that the place could be improved by a new piece of furniture. The settler likes his place just the way it is. It's comfortable. It's predictable. It's a nice safe place to spend a whole lifetime. The trouble is, Jesus keeps talking about taking up crosses and bearing other's burdens and going into all the world, which is hard to do from your living room sofa.

▶ Inter Action

The Pilgrim/Settler Quiz

For each of the following questions, circle the answer that most nearly fits your situation. Circle only one answer for each question or it will throw off the scoring mechanism at the end.

Answer the questions in terms of how you are actually living rather than in terms of how you would like to be living, think you should be living, or plan to live in the future. (Of course, when a question refers to a situation which is hypothetical for you, then you have to respond in terms of how you think you would act, if you were actually in that situation.)

One final note: This quiz is an indicator of life-style, not an examination or an absolute definition of right or wrong ways of living. It will not determine whether you are a good Christian or a bad Christian. No value judgments of any sort are intended. It is merely a vehicle which hopefully will provide useful insights for you personally. (If you are concerned about others seeing your answers, mark your response in your notebook and not below.) Have fun with it!

1. How often, when you hear about a new book or an important article, do you actually get the book or article and read it?
   a) Occasionally
   b) Seldom
   c) Never

2. Have you ever considered joining an encounter group of some sort?
   a) Yes, seriously
   b) Thought about it
   c) Never

3. Who do you pay attention to when they speak of Christian things?
   a) A number of people
   b) Several people
   c) One person, mainly

4. How do you feel when new people join your church?
   a) Excited
   b) Glad but cautious
   c) A bit uneasy

5. Do you ever pay attention to a dream you have had?
   a) Yes
   b) Rarely
   c) Never

6. How do you (or did you at first) feel when you see the Hari Krishna chanting in a park or near the department stores?
   a) Wonder what it is that attracts kids to this group
   b) Mildly curious but quickly forget about them
   c) Angry that an eastern sect should have been imported

7. How many different periodicals (magazines, newspapers, etc.) do you read each month?
   a) Eight or more
   b) Three to seven
   c) Two or less

8. When was the last conference or retreat you attended?
   a) Less than six months ago
   b) Six months to one year ago
   c) Over a year ago

9. When you study the Bible, do you:
   a) Consult various translations
   b) Use one or two translations
   c) Use one translation almost exclusively

10. Apart from church activities, are you involved in other activities as a result of your Christian convictions?
    a) Yes
    b) Have been in the past
    c) No

11. When was the last time you had, in one way or another, a sense of God's presence or leading?
    a) Just recently
    b) A while ago
    c) Never

12. How often do you watch the educational channel on TV?
    a) Often
    b) Occasionally
    c) Seldom

13. When did you last take a study course of some sort?
    a) Recently
    b) A while ago
    c) A long time ago

14. How often do you feel restless about your growth as a Christian and then do something concrete about it?
    a) Occasionally
    b) Seldom
    c) Never

15. When was the last time you went to a special lecture or discussion?
    a) Within the last three months
    b) Within the last year
    c) Over a year ago

16. How do you react when a Jehovah's Witness visits you?
    a) Listen carefully to him and interact (at least the first visit)
    b) Listen politely but think little about what is said
    c) Listen but all the time say to yourself, "He is so misguided!"

17. In thinking about the boundaries of your life, would you consider them:
    a) Fluid
    b) Fixed but expanding slowly
    c) Fairly fixed

18. When did you last undertake a creative project?
    a) Recently
    b) A while ago
    c) A long time ago

19. Do you find Christian fellowship and support:
    a) From a variety of sources
    b) At several places
    c) At one place mainly

20. Think of the last three books you read—were they:
    a) On different subjects
    b) On the same subject
    c) Haven't read three books in a long time

21. Of the people you invite into your home, are they:
    a) From a variety of different backgrounds
    b) Mostly Christian friends and occasionally others
    c) Generally Christian friends

22. How do you feel about people who are very active in a church quite different from your own?
    a) Good
    b) Unsure
    c) Feel somewhat sorry for them that they are not in a better church

23. In terms of your attitudes, do you consider yourself:
    a) Able to change some of these

b) Pretty stable
c) Growing more fixed

Scoring

Now count up all the "a's" and enter below. Do the same for the "b's" and the "c's". Then multiply each as indicated and total your score. Finally, put an "x" on the number line below where your total falls.

No. of a's = _____ × 3 = _____

No. of b's = _____ × 2 = _____

No. of c's = _____ × 1 = _____

TOTAL = _____

Settler ├ 25 30 35 40 45 50 55 60 65 70 75 ┤ Pilgrim

Needless to say, this is hardly a scientifically constructed quiz. Nor does it adequately take into account the unique situation of each person. And yet, I do think it will give a useful indication of where a person is in terms of being a pilgrim or a settler. If you are near the settler end of the scale, you need to start becoming sensitive to the boundaries of your life and how you are relating to them. If you are near the pilgrim end of the scale, you'll welcome the opportunity to gain some new insights for the next step in your walk. In either case, I hope that the pages which follow will prove useful.

▶ Inter Action

Pilgrim Images

Before embarking on this chapter, it would be profitable for you to spend a few moments reflecting on your own inner image of a pilgrim. Images are powerful forces in our lives, affecting our thinking, feeling, and reacting, and so it is important to be in touch with them on a conscious level.

I. Close your eyes and think about the word "pilgrim." How do you understand that word? What images come to mind? Can you visualize a pilgrim? What does he/she look like? Act like? In what surroundings does a pilgrim live? Let these images assume shape in your mind.

II. After a few minutes, try to crystalize your image of a pilgrim:

A. By drawing a picture, abstract or realistic.

B. Or by writing about what you see. Don't worry about aesthetic skill when you do this. The aim is to make your mental image more concrete so that you can deal with it, not to develop your writing or drawing ability.

III. Think about this image:

A. Is your image of a pilgrim positive or negative? Does it attract or repel you? Why?

B. Can you see yourself as a pilgrim? Why or why not?

I have a friend for whom the word "pilgrim" instantly connotes "groveling, ignorant, superstitious peasants crawling up to dingy religious shrines to kiss the feet of a wooden Jesus." You can imagine how difficult it was at first for him to get involved in a Bible study we were having on the theme of pilgrims in biblical literature. If your image of the pilgrim is also negative, you will want to be alert to your reactions as you read the following chapter. How you feel about pilgrims and pilgrimage will pre-condition what you read in this book.

2 The Pilgrim

I have long been intrigued by the image of the pilgrim. For me, he has always been a tall, gaunt individual: weather-hardened, rugged, possessing only what he could carry in his back pack. I see him on top of a ridge, resting on a wooden staff, looking out across the land with deep, penetrating eyes. He is a serious individual, interested only in what is real and true. He has little time for pretense. He is not, however, without humor. In fact, his laugh is rich, deep, and spontaneous.

He is on a journey. It is an important journey and one he has undertaken only after long and careful consideration. Now he is totally dedicated to it. He does not pursue his goal with frenzied haste. He moves deliberately and steadily, yet he seems to have ample time to enjoy what he encounters along the way—flowers, children, fresh grass, the sun, villagers, great libraries, and lonely caves.

My pilgrim is a dedicated man. He has been called to persevere until he reaches his goal and he has willingly put all else aside to follow this solitary path. He knows he will not reach this goal quickly. In fact, he is on a pilgrimage that will take a lifetime. Yet there is no impatience in him. He simply keeps moving, buoyed by the sure sense that one day he will arrive and that then he will find treasure beyond imagining.

I am not at all sure where this picture comes from. The figure himself, as best I can tell, is an amalgam of various images: a knight from King Arthur's Round Table, the character in old woodcuts from *Pilgrim's Progress,* Charlton Heston in one of his biblical roles, and Saint Francis of Assisi.

The land this pilgrim treads is agrarian in nature—full of cultivated fields, forests, streams, and mountains. The era he lives in is medieval. It is a time of peasants, thatch houses, hard work, isolated centers of learning, and simple pleasures. It is an age in which evil is present, but well-defined, and very concrete. It is an age of great deeds.

17

For me, this is a very positive, very powerful image. It symbolizes a life which is deeply satisfying—a single-minded pursuit of a significant goal which is undertaken because one is called to do so. It is not an easy life. The journey is long and hard, and fraught with very real dangers which must be overcome. But it is a life lived in touch with elemental realities, and thus is deeply fulfilling.

This image is not my private property. In fact, the pilgrim (or hero) is among the most common and best-known myths in the world. It has occurred in one form or another in cultures as different as those of ancient Greece and the Winnebago Indians. According to C. G. Jung, this image has its origin in an *archetype* which Jung defines as "an irrepresentable, unconscious, pre-existent form that seems to be part of the inherited structure of the psyche and can therefore manifest itself spontaneously anywhere, at any time."[1] Arising as it does out of our fundamental nature, the pilgrim image has the power to "impress, influence, and fascinate us."[2] It can set up within us strange longings and call forth powerful emotions, and therefore is able to influence us deeply. Evelyn Underhill, in her classic work, *Mysticism,* notes that the pilgrim image appeals to that deep craving of the self which "makes (a man) a pilgrim and wanderer. It is the longing to go out from his normal world in search of a lost home, a 'better country;' an Eldorado, a Heavenly Zion."[3]

It is not surprising, therefore, that the idea of a pilgrimage has assumed a central role in a variety of religions down through the ages. I recall being in Nairobi International Airport on one occasion when a planeload of Muslims arrived from Saudi-Arabia. They had been on a pilgrimage to Mecca. The whole scene still remains with me: the airport terminal crowded with friends and family eager to greet and embrace each returning pilgrim; the smiles, the noise and the enthusiasm of everyone; the obvious poverty of many of the disembarking passengers. Here were men and women who had saved for an entire lifetime to make this one journey. Even today, in Islam, a pilgrimage to Mecca is seen as the culmination of a lifetime of devotion.

The idea of pilgrimage is also a central concept in the Old Testament. It was by means of a pilgrimage that the nation of Israel began. Abraham left his home in Ur and ventured out into the unknown because God called him to do so, the end result of which was the founding of a new nation. It was by means of another pilgrimage that this nation, now quite large, left its slavery and came into a land of its own. Even today the Exodus from Egypt is remembered and celebrated.

As it turned out, the Children of Israel learned great and permanent lessons during the long years they spent wandering in the wilderness. They learned that God kept His promises; they learned that He would sustain them as a nation under the most adverse of circumstances; they learned of God's law and the Ten Commandments became the pillar upon which the nation developed. It was in the wilderness that they developed the fundamental structures of nationhood which were to serve them well in later ages. God could have led them directly from Egypt to the Promised Land in a matter of months. The distance was not great. But Israel needed all those years in the wilderness as a pilgrim people in order to discover the unique thing that God was making out of them.

So it is that this image of the pilgrim was forever impressed upon the minds of the people of Israel. It is not surprising therefore that the writer of "The Letter to the Hebrews" chose to remind the Jewish Christians of their calling to be pilgrims, and in the process defined the pilgrim as a model for all Christians. This New Testament image of the pilgrim contained some important differences, however. No longer was the journey seen as purely physical. For the Christian, the journey is much more inward, involving growth in his perceptions, his relationships, and his actions—in short, growth in the whole of his life. Nor is our journey completed in a specific period of time. Rather, it involves a whole lifetime. Our goal is different, too. Though as real and concrete as Mecca or the Promised Land, the New Jerusalem is not geographical in nature. Rather it symbolizes for us wholeness and God's presence, both of which will one day be ours.

I believe there are at least three distinguishing marks that characterize a Christian pilgrim. The first, and perhaps most distinctive quality, is that of *movement*. A pilgrim is an individual who has embarked on a journey of growth. Second, a pilgrim is characterized by his awareness of a *goal*. He is not involved in aimless wandering but rather in progressing purposefully toward a very distinctive, very real objective. Finally, a pilgrim is characterized by his *willingness to pay the price* such a life-style requires. He keeps moving toward his goal, despite the difficulty and pain that this sometimes involves.

Movement

As the very image itself connotes, the pilgrim is a man in motion. He is an individual who is restless to learn. To my mind, it is this restlessness which sets a modern pilgrim apart from his fellows, who all too often live their whole lives based solely on what they learn in the early years of life. The pilgrim does not disparage the truths he learned while growing into adulthood, but rather yearns to find out what lies behind them, why they are true, how they apply in different areas of life. He wants to understand as much about them as he can. He wants to live them and experience them. Truth, for the pilgrim, is not a static statement. It is more like a many-faceted jewel which when held up to the light reveals ever new configurations and colors. The pilgrim longs to get to the essence of what is true in all its multi-faceted brilliance.

"But," some will say, "while this may be OK for folk wisdom, surely Christian truth is fixed and certain. To know what is true is to know it.

To seek to go beyond is to open oneself to heresy." While it is true that certain men and women have taken basic Christian truths and elaborated on them in such a way as to make them unrecognizable, these flights of fancy are not what I am talking about. It is one thing to distort a truth into something new and different from the original. It is quite another to seek to know in depth as much as one can about a particular truth.

Take, for example, the doctrine of the atonement. The essence of this doctrine is summed up in the phrase "Christ died for our sins." This is simple enough. Countless people down through the ages have trusted that this was so and as a result found peace with God. And yet, innumerable books, papers and treatises, both learned and popular, have been written about the atonement. In my own library I have twenty books dealing with this one subject, and scores of others which touch upon it. Just last week, a publisher sent me my twenty-first volume on the subject—a brand new book on one aspect of the atonement!

How can this be? All these words about such a straightforward affirmation? But this is the point. The doctrine of the atonement is at once both utterly simple and totally profound. And for a Christian to know this doctrine only in its simplicity is a tragedy. This is to live on the surface and never to penetrate to the depths. The pilgrim, however, is ever yearning to know and understand in deeper ways.

But a pilgrim is not simply content to *know about* a truth. He wants to live it as well. He wants that doctrine to be incarnated in his very life and experience. Because Christ died for our sins, we can really and truly be forgiven, and the pilgrim seeks to learn to *live* as a forgiven man. This is not an easy thing to do. It is only gradually that we come to *experience* forgiveness. And as we grow in this personal experience, so, too, we grow in our ability to forgive others. Our relationships therefore begin to change as we learn to accept others in the same way in which God accepts us. This is the work of a lifetime, not something that happens automatically the moment we first affirm our trust in Christ's atoning death.

For the pilgrim, learning is all-embracing, touching on every facet of his life—his mind, his emotions, his sensations, his will, his intuition, his attitudes, and his behaviour. He wants to grow in understanding and wisdom. He wants to widen the range of his experience. He seeks to develop new and ever more healthy attitudes and emotions. He wants to sharpen his spiritual intuitions. Since such all-encompassing growth is not accomplished in a moment, the pilgrim can be content to learn one thing at a time. He can focus his attention on one area for awhile and then move on to a new area. He has no compulsion to know everything immediately, because he knows his learning will be a lifelong experience and he can afford patiently to pursue learning in depth.

This patient growth contrasts sharply with the almost compulsive way new Christians are pushed at times to adopt a Christian life-style, as if this can be accomplished overnight. Not only does this put all sorts of unnatural pressures on the convert, but it also causes us to lower our expectations. A "good Christian" is seen as a person who subscribes to a certain set of doctrines, who attends church regularly, and who does *not* do certain forbidden things (such as getting drunk) because you cannot expect much more of a person in a short time. Instant growth is necessarily stunted growth. When we make it normative, the whole body of Christ suffers.

The same mentality which sees growth as what happens at the very beginning of one's Christian life is also responsible, I think, for the mad pursuit after new Christian "gurus" that one witnesses in America. Anyone who promises a quick and easy path to spiritual knowledge and experience is guaranteed a following. The pilgrim knows, however, that there is no substitute for patient perseverance, and is content to let God teach him one thing at a time.

Reflecting on my own experience, it is clear that over the years my attention has been focused first on one area and then another. For example, as a teen-ager, most of my Christian growth seemed to be concentrated on understanding how to perceive the world around me in spiritual terms. At that time in my life, I had to learn the difference between certain cultural perspectives I had always held (because everyone held them) and Christian perspectives which were quite new and different. I had assumed, prior to my Christian commitment, that my goal in life was to get educated in order to qualify for a secure, well-paying job which would insure a life of abundance. I came to see, however, that if the Kingdom of God were real, then security and abundance could not be the main focus of one's attentions. Rather, spreading the good news of the reality of this Kingdom had to have a priority.

When I was in seminary and during my first years in Africa, my growth was more focused on deepening my understanding of my Christian faith. I can remember the unexpected joy one day when I was studying for an exam in systematic theology and suddenly *understood* in a whole new way what the doctrine of atonement was all about. I had believed in the atonement for years, but then I knew what it meant in a totally new way. I also remember the long hours of preparation for university missions during which I immersed myself in historical apologetics until finally I understood how strong the evidence was that Jesus was indeed God-come-in-human-flesh. It was a startling discovery and one that has since become a bedrock of my faith.

Now at this point in my life, I have been drawn inextricably to new understanding and experiences of my inner nature. I am discovering whole new vistas of spiritual reality I had never before dreamed existed.

There is a beautiful section at the end of *The Last Battle* which captures the essence of the movement we should seek in our Christian life. A great doorway opens up in Narnia through which the children and the animals pass. They discover on the other side that they have come into the true Narnia, the reality behind the shadow which they always understood to be Narnia itself. It is the Unicorn that announces this discovery: "I have come home at last," he declares. "This is my real country! I belong here. This is the land I have been looking for all my life though I never knew it til now. The reason why we loved the old Narnia is that it sometimes looked a little like this."[4]

Yet even this land proves but the shadow of still another Narnia that lies within. It is here that Lucy realizes: "This is still Narnia, and, more and more beautiful than the Narnia down below, just as *it* was more real and more beautiful than the Narnia outside the stable door! I see . . . world within world, Narnia within Narnia . . ."[5]

The pilgrim too journeys further up and further in, never exhausting God's truth, only discovering more and more the wonder of it, always finding it bigger and richer than he had ever imagined, finding that he is coming more and more in touch with truer and truer reality. How sad to be found one day sitting at the borders of Narnia, announcing to one and all that you have discovered true reality, but really only knowing this intellectually, having never journeyed much more than a few paces into that glorious country. There is a very high price to be paid for remaining a settler.

A Goal

There is a second distinguishing characteristic of a pilgrim. He has a goal toward which he journeys.

Abraham's goal was a new land where God would make of him a great nation. The writer to the Hebrews says that all Old Testament pilgrims shared this desire for "a better country, that is a heavenly one." Saint John, in his raptures in the Book of Revelation, describes this new place which constitutes the goal of all true pilgrims:

> Then I saw a new heaven and a new earth; for the first heaven and the first earth had passed away, and the sea was no more. And I saw the holy city, new Jerusalem, coming down out of heaven from God, prepared as a bride adorned for her husband; and I heard a great voice from the throne saying, "Behold, the dwelling of God is with men. He will dwell with them, and they shall be his people and God himself shall be with them; he will wipe away every tear from their eyes, and death shall be no more, neither shall there be mourning nor crying nor pain any more, for the former things have passed away." And he who sat upon the throne said, "Behold, I make all things new." (Rev. 21:1-5a)

And what characterizes the New Jerusalem? First and foremost, it is the presence of God. This fact is so astounding that John repeats it three times in one verse: "Behold, the dwelling of God is with men. He will dwell with them, and they shall be his people, and God himself will be with them." The pilgrim's goal is the presence of God.

Hence the passion with which Saint Bernard can write of the City of Zion:

> Oh Zion, thou city sole and single, mystic mansion hidden away in the heavens, now I rejoice in thee, now I moan for thee and mourn and yearn for thee; thee often I pass through in the heart, as I cannot in the body, but being of earthly flesh and fleshly earth soon I fall back. None can disclose or utter in speech what plenary radiance fills thy walls and thy citadels. I can as little tell of it as I can touch the skies with my finger, or run upon the sea or make a dart stand still in the air. This thy splendor overwhelms my every heart, O Zion, O Peace! O timeless City, no praise can belie thee. O new dwelling-place, thee the concourse and people of the faithful erects and exalts, inspires and increases, joins to itself, and makes complete and one.[6]

But this is not all. The pilgrim's goal is also characterized by personal wholeness. Saint John tells us that the afflictions we now have—pain, tears, suffering, mourning, and even death itself, will pass away. Sin will no longer reign and man will be freed from the imperfections which so weigh him down. He will *be* what God intended him to be right from the beginning. The ravages of his fallen nature will be past. He will be whole.

This is not to say, however, that the pilgrim must await the completion of his journey before he experiences the presence of God or knows the meaning of wholeness. Along the way there are hints and intimations of what it means to dwell in God's presence. The pilgrim reads of men like Abraham, Moses and David who knew God. He listens to Jesus describe the Kingdom of God. He hears his contemporaries witness to life-shattering encounters with God. But, most significantly of all, he experiences those moments, however brief, when the veil is pulled aside and he knows God in the very depths of his own being.

Likewise, he begins to experience the meaning of wholeness. He finds that he is growing as a person. He is beginning to *lose* certain traits that plague him. He finds, perhaps, that his temper is less than it used to be. He also discovers that he is *developing* new traits. He is more patient and loving now. He is, in fact, in the process of becoming what God calls him to be — a whole person.

It is this matter of a goal that marks the difference between a pilgrim and a spiritual vagabond. From time to time one meets those individuals who bustle from spiritual concern to spiritual concern. One month they are hyperactive in a *koininia* group. The next month they are enthusiastic charismatics. In a short time they drop this interest and get involved in organizing a boycott. Here is activity and movement, but it is undirected. The spiritual vagabond flits from activity to activity, searching, almost desperately, for meaning, for "spiritual thrills," or for an experience that will make him "better" than someone else. He is not in touch yet with what God wants to bring about in his life. Until that happens, his activity will never become a pilgrimage.

This consciousness of goal very much affects how the pilgrim lives his daily life. A man who believes that his life will one day be abruptly terminated by death with nothing beyond it, decides quite differently from the pilgrim how he invests his time, how he relates to other people and to the needs of the world, how he uses his money, even how he will face death. The pilgrim who believes that death merely marks a transition from an earthly life to an after life lived in God's presence, invests his energies in ways that relate to the Kingdom of God, at times doing what appears quite foolish when judged by the non-pilgrim ethic. He might give up an established career in physics to become pastor of a small and (seemingly) insignificant church. Or he might be found spending his evenings in the inner city tutoring children, or perhaps in his study praying and meditating.

The pilgrim has a goal: to dwell in the presence of God as a whole person. It is a goal that draws him ever onward. At times this goal is dim and half-forgotten. But then come those moments of insight and knowing; and his goal is crystal clear once again. But dim or clear, the goal is very real to him. He cannot escape the restless longing to grasp it. He is indeed lured by things beyond.

The Price

But the life of pilgrimage is not without its price. By its very nature a journey forward necessitates a leaving behind. And it is this *leaving behind* which constitutes the hardship of pilgrimage. It could not have been easy for Abraham to leave the high civilization of Chaldea. Yet without this renunciation he would never have come into the land of promise.

The nature of this *leaving behind* varies throughout our lifetime. There are moments when we are called upon to leave behind certain presuppositions of our culture and face the misunderstanding and even ridicule of our peers. At other times, we may have to leave behind a particular Christian group that has meant so much to us, simply because we know that by staying we would be limiting our growth, and failing to move in the new directions to which God has called us. We may be asked to leave behind the comfort and security of our present job in order to launch out into a new venture. Or we may have to leave behind certain attitudes or ideas which have proved to be inadequate. And in the process we may be leaving behind friends who are still comfortable living with those perceptions.

Whatever its nature, it is not easy to leave anything behind. There is a certain comfort and security to the "known," whereas the "new" to which we are being called cannot help but be a bit frightening. Nowhere in Scripture is pilgrimage pictured as invariably easy. In fact, Hebrews 11:35b-38 is positively chilling: "Some were tortured, refusing to accept release, that they might rise again to a better life. Others suffered mocking and scourging, and even chains and imprisonment. They were stoned, they were sawn in two, they were killed with the sword; they went about in skins of sheep and goats, destitute, afflicted, ill-treated—of whom the world was not worthy—wandering over deserts and mountains, and in dens and caves of the earth." Perhaps it is the fear that we also may be asked to pay a high price that stops many of us from moving out of our settled life to a life of pilgrimage. The life of the settler, after all, seems to offer security and insulation from the uglier things in life. But it too has its price: the price of living on the surface of one's faith; the price of failing to claim the riches of our inheritance; the price of disobeying God; and the price of experiencing sheer boredom.

But let us not think that pilgrimage is all agony. There is a price to be paid, to be sure, but there are also great rewards; and it has been a mistake of the church at times to stress the hardship without mentioning the hope. Perhaps the words of Paul Pruyser, a psychiatrist at the Menninger Clinic, are appropriate for the beginning of a pilgrimage:

> ". . . the larger part of the road to holiness consists in enormous satisfactions, good feelings, and a deep sense of well-being shared with friends, if not with the whole universe."[7]

▶ Inter Action

Strangers and Pilgrims:
A Study of Hebrews 11:13-16

The founding fathers of Israel, Abraham, Isaac and Jacob, were pilgrims in the literal sense. In Gen. 12:1, God says to Abraham: "Go from your country and your kindred and your father's house to the land that I will show you." Abraham obeyed, and thus Israel's history began with a pilgrimage. During this journey, God tells Abraham that not only he, but also his descendents will be sojourners: "Know of a surety that your descendents will be sojourners." (Gen. 15:13) When the pilgrimage led Israel to Egypt and slavery, God raised up Moses who led them out of that land and into the wilderness and so the journey continued.

In the New Testament, Jesus led the life of a pilgrim, wandering in his ministry "through the towns and villages, teaching and journeying towards Jerusalem" (Luke 13:22). As he himself said: "Foxes have holes, and birds of the air have nests; but the Son of Man has nowhere to lay his head" (Matt. 8:20). Thus the writer to the Hebrews can conclude his list of Old Testament pilgrims by pointing to Jesus as "the pioneer and the perfecter of our faith"—the one who has led the way on this journey—and has done so perfectly (Heb. 12:2).

Although the image of the Christian life as a "pilgrim's progress" is found throughout the Bible, it is in the book of Hebrews that this concept is given its most complete expression. Here the parallel is drawn between Israel having been saved from Egypt and then brought through the desert toward the promised land of Canaan; and Christians having been saved from sin, travelling as aliens and exiles through this life toward the "New Jerusalem," where they will find the wholeness and rest they have been promised.

This pilgrim image finds focus particularly in Heb. 11:13-16. However, this passage is set in the context of Hebrews 11 itself with its definition of faith and illustration of this definition in the lives of Old Testament heroes. In fact, this whole section of thought probably begins at 10:32 and ends only at the close of Chapter 12. It is important therefore that some time is spent getting a sense of the context which surrounds verses 13-16, before looking at these key verses in detail. Use your notebook to answer the following questions.

I. The Context: Read quickly Hebrews 10:32 - 12:29.

A. Hebrews 10:32-39. This section focuses on experience of the Hebrew Christians to whom the letter is addressed.

1. What did they go through?

2. How did they react to these problems?

3. How do you think you might react if one day men came to your house and demanded to know if you were a Christian, and when you answered "yes," they confiscated your home and all you owned, turning you and your family out into the street?

4. What is the danger these Christians now face?

5. What qualities do they have need of?

6. Notice verse 38a. It sets the stage for Chapter 11. How could you paraphrase (*i.e.*, put into your own words) verse 38a?

B. The author now moves from the recent experience of these Hebrew Christians to consider the past experience of Old Testament heroes, in order to search out truths that will be of value to these people as they face the temptation to drift away from their hard-bought faith.

1. In Hebrews 10:38a, the author has indicated that *faith* is the key to living successfully as a Christian. He begins Chapter 11 by defining what he means by faith.

a. Notice the double aspect of faith as defined in 11:1. Which part of the definition points to the future? Which points to the present?

b. According to 11:2, what is one reward of faith? Notice how verse two relates to "the assurance of things hoped for."

c. Notice, then, how verse three relates to "the conviction of things not seen." Where is real reality and how do we apprehend it?

2. The writer now moves to illustrate how this forward-looking faith provides the key to living in this world. His point seems to be that the pilgrim way is not an untrodden path. It has been prepared for us by a host of Old Testament figures and by Jesus himself.

a. Note and underline each time the phrase "by faith" appears in Chapter 11.

b. Read through Heb. 11:4-12 and 11:7-12:2, noting with each new illustration how faith, as defined in verse one, provides a vital element in that person's experience. What recurring themes do you note in these sections? Make a list.

c. Note in 11:6 the emphasis on the two aspects of faith.

d. In 12:1 and 2, what is the new but parallel metaphor which is introduced?

II. The Passage

These all died in faith, not having received what was promised, but having seen it and greeted it from afar, and having acknowledged that they were strangers and exiles on the earth. For people who speak thus make it clear that they are seeking a homeland. If they had been thinking of that land from which they had gone out, they would have had opportunity to return. But as it is, they desire a better country, that is, a heavenly one. Therefore God is not ashamed to be called their God, for he has prepared for them a city. (Heb. 11:13-16 RSV)

A. Verse 13.

1. The phrase "these all" probably refers only to the patriarchs, Abraham and his wife Sarah, Isaac and Jacob, mentioned in the previous paragraph; not to the first three heroes listed, since it is stated that Enoch had not experienced death.

2. What promises had they been given? How do we today see so much more clearly the fulfillment of these promises?

3. What phrases are used to describe the relationship of the patriarchs to the promises?

a. The image here is fascinating. Picture the desert and the colorful tents of the patriarch pitched around a camp. He stands, a solitary individual, gazing out across the shimmering heat of the desert. Are those soaring towers and flying pennants that keep coming in and out of focus there in the far distance? Perhaps, perhaps. In any case, he will keep on journeying because God has told him that indeed there is a city where he belongs.

b. Have you ever experienced any "glimpses of reality" at points in your Christian walk? Describe some of these intimations.

c. Think about the difference between glimpses and constant vision. Think about the relation between faith and sight; and our temptation to want to live by sight when in fact we are called to live by faith. Is this 'temptation to sight' one of the factors involved in adopting a settler's life-style whereby we live within the confines of "what we know assuredly to be true" rather than walking by faith toward an as yet unrealized goal?

d. The Greek words translated here "strangers and exiles" ("strangers and pilgrims" in the King James version) are interesting. *Xenos* is the Greek word for a foreigner or a stranger. In the ancient world, foreigners and stranges were greeted with suspicion and contempt. When the tribe was all the security an individual had, he guarded it jealously. Who knew why these aliens were here? Perhaps they were spies? Foreigners were never really accepted into an alient culture. The second word, *parepidemos*, was used for a person staying temporarily at a place but whose real home was elsewhere. To be an exile was a humiliating experience.[8]

Think about the first time you travelled to a foreign land (if you have), especially one in which you did not know the language. Try to image living *for the rest of your life* with the confusion, the difficulty, the lack of belonging you experience in modern day "culture shock" and add to this the suspicion, humiliation, and even hatred an exile faced in ancient days, and you begin to get a feel for what the Patriarchs endured.

B. Verses 14-16. These verses amplify the final phrases of verse 13: "they acknowledged that they were strangers and exiles."

1. For what reason did they endure life as pilgrims?

2. "Home" for them was Mesopotamia, the so-called Cradle of Civilization. Abraham did not leave the primitive backwaters to seek fame and fortune in rich lands. He left the heart of civilization to journey into the unknown.

3. There is a difference between a nomad and a pilgrim. A nomad simply wanders. A pilgrim has a goal. What was the goal for the patriarchs? See Heb. 11:10, 14, 16 and 12:22; and Rev. 21:1-5a. Using these references, describe the characteristics of this goal. Notice the two strata present here: Jerusalem is an actual city with a geographical location. It is the shadow of the "real" Jerusalem described in Rev. 21.

4. What do we learn of God's nature in verse 16?

5. What is the goal in our own pilgrimage?

III. Implications. Thinking back on what you have read and studied, and on the exercises you have done thus far, try to draw together your thoughts by developing a list of the characteristics of a pilgrimage. You ought to be able to come up with at least seven such characteristics (besides the three described in detail in Chapter 2).

3   The Psychology of Growth

When we speak of pilgrims and settlers, of the price of pilgrimage and the danger of settling down, of the New Jerusalem as our goal, we are using biblical images. We are speaking out of a theological framework. This is a problem to some people, because lurking in the back of their minds is the question: "Yes, but is this *just* theology?" i.e., Is this something which is true only in the framework of faith?

I think it is a sad commentary on the state of theology that it has become so disconnected in our minds with life and truth that such a question is even asked. Nevertheless it is, and because this is so, it is useful to look at what another discipline has to say about these same issues. After all, if the God of our faith is indeed the Creator who made us and our world, then His footprints should be discernable by unbiased empirical observers. Accordingly, let us turn to psychology, since it is the discipline which is concerned with human growth.*

Surprisingly, psychologists have not always been interested in human growth, at least not in the development of normal, healthy individuals. In fact, in its infancy, scientific psychology seemed far more interested in sick individuals than healthy ones. The reason for this is that many of the early psychologists were medical doctors (e.g., Freud and Jung) and their interest in psychology was clinical in nature. They turned to psychology in order to learn how to heal individuals who were suffering from diseases for which no physical cause could be discerned. Only later did

---

*In the discussion which follows, when I refer to "psychology" or "the findings of psychology," I am, of course, not referring to the settled convictions of the whole discipline. No such consensus exists on virtually any issue. What I intend to show is that there is a significant and reputable stream within the total discipline which treats man's nature in much the same way as does the Bible.

psychology turn from its preoccupation with abnormal psychology and begin investigating healthy individuals in order to understand the dynamics of normal growth.

One of the men who has contributed much to our understanding of normal growth is Abraham Maslow, former Chairman of the Graduate Department of Psychology at Brandeis University. In 1950, Maslow published a paper detailing his studies of "self-actualizing people."[1] Actually, the paper was written in 1943, but it took him seven years to get up the courage to publish it. His reluctance stemmed from the fact that what he discusses is not a research project in the orthodox sense, with sampling techniques and nicely worked out statistical analysis. Nor was he treating what at that time would have been considered an orthodox subject for inquiry. In fact, this research began as a purely personal project in which Maslow sought to satisfy himself as to why certain intriguing individuals seemed to be able to live life to the full, and to manifest a zeal, an enthusiasm, and a creativeness in relationship to living, which is quite different from what most of us seem able to muster. He wanted to identify what caused this zest for living which was at once so desirable and yet so rare.

Maslow points out that the study proved more difficult than expected. For one thing, he had trouble finding the right subjects for his inquiry. In screening 3,000 college students he located only one he could use in his research. (He later concluded that self-actualization of the sort he was looking for was not really found in young, still-developing students.) Maslow found that the older subjects he really needed to use "when informed of the purpose of the research, became self-conscious, froze up, laughed off the whole effort, or broke off the relationship."[2] Apparently, part of what is involved in being a self-actualized individual is an unawareness that one is living and growing in a way substantially different from others. As a result, all of his older subjects had to be studied indirectly, indeed "almost surreptitiously," as Maslow put it. Only the younger (and less ideal) subjects could be interviewed directly. In addition, Maslow included public and historical figures (*e.g.,* Einstein and Freud) in his study.

What Maslow sought were people who were free from neurosis, psychosis and other personality disorders, and who made "full use and exploitation of talents, capacities, potentialities, etc. Such people seem to be fulfilling themselves and to be doing the best that they are capable of doing. . . ."[3]

The first thing that Maslow did was to develop a profile of the self-actualized individual. He found thirteen distinctive characteristics.

1. Superior perception of reality.
2. Increased acceptance of self, of others, and of nature.
3. Increased spontaneity.
4. Increase in problem-centering.

5. Increased detachment and desire for privacy.
6. Increased autonomy, and resistance to enculturation.
7. Greater freshness of appreciation, and richness of emotional reaction.
8. Higher frequency of peak experiences.
9. Increased identification with the human species.
10. Changed (the clinician would say, improved) interpersonal relations.
11. More democratic character structure.
12. Greatly increased creativeness.
13. Certain changes in the value system.[4]

Eventually Maslow defined the self-actualized individual as one in whom there was an "ongoing actualization of potentials, capabilities and talents; a fulfillment of mission (or call, fate, destiny, or vocation); a fuller knowledge of, and acceptance of, the person's own intrinsic nature; and an increasing trend toward unity, integration or synergy within the person."[5]

This sounds much like the sort of person we have been defining as a pilgrim: an individual who is striving and growing; who is realizing ('actualizing' is Maslow's word) more and more of his unique God-given potential; who is aware of God's leading for his life and walking faithfully along this path; in short, a person who is becoming all God intends him to be. Not only did this study recognize and note the value of such growth, it revealed something else which is relevant to our concerns. It lent confirmation to Maslow's contention that there really is "some sort of positive growth or self-actualization tendency within the organism, which is different from its conserving, equilibrating, or homeostatic tendency, as well as from the tendency to respond to impulses from the outside world."[6] In other words, the human organism "develops from within by intrinsic growth tendencies . . . rather than from without, in the behavioristic sense of environmental determinism."[7] He goes on, "self-actualization is intrinsic growth of what is already in the organism, or more accurately of what *is* the organism itself."[8] And, ". . . full health and normal and desirable development consists in actualizing (man's essential) nature, in fulfilling these potentialities, and in developing into maturity along the lines that this hidden, covert, dimly seen essential nature dictates, going from within rather than being shaped from without."[9]

What Maslow has pin-pointed (along with other writers such as Goldstein, Jung, Adler, Horney, Fromm, May and Rogers) is the fact that there is within man himself (his "essential nature" Maslow would call it) a "sense" of the directions along which he is meant to develop. Others would put this even more strongly. Edmund Sinnott, the biologist, feels that built into the very protoplasm of our cells is "a tendency to develop toward a given end." We are not, in other words, passive victims of our environment who can become only what our circumstances dictate (though no one would deny environmental influence). Built into our very natures is a purpose and a goal. Finding that purpose and goal, and then living in accord with its dictates is what is necessary to becoming fully human. Those who do this (Maslow calls them self-actualizing individuals) are distinguishable by the very zest they bring to living.

All this accords nicely with what has been said so far about pilgrimage. In fact, I see the image of pilgrimage as a metaphor for this very self-actualizing process. To stop growing, to settle down in a comfortable 'position,' is to fail in following the purpose built into our very cellular structure (if Sinnott is right). It is to decide to remain less than we could be or were meant to be.

The Christian perspective adds a further dimension to Maslow's insights. It posits that as part of this pilgrimage process it is vital that a man come to grips with the most fundamental rupture in his nature (between himself and God) and be reconciled with God in order that he both experience and live in fellowship with Him.

It is interesting that Maslow has noted the 'spiritual dimension' in the self-actualizing process, although he does not state this in the specifically Christian terms I have used.* As he writes: "Those subjective expressions that have been called the mystic experience and described so well by William James (in *The Varieties of Religious Experience*) are a fairly common experience for our subjects (my italics)."[11]

Maslow is not alone in this recognition that the spiritual plays a vital part in man's growth toward meaning. Ira Progoff, in summarizing where four of the pioneers in the development of depth psychology ended up in regard to their understanding of man's nature, writes these remarkable words:

> They were led to an experience of the spiritual core of man's being, to the seed of personality that unfolds psychologically in each person and yet is always more than psychological. They came, in other words, to the metaphysical foundation of life that underlies psychology; and since each one experienced it in a personal way, each gave it a different name. Freud spoke of it as the superego accepting the ego, a characteristically intellectual way to describe a basic cosmic experience. Adler called it "social feeling," and through it he gained a profound and intimate connection to life. Jung referred to it as the "individuation" of the "Self," an abstract phrase to describe his effort to experience the cosmos psychologically by means of symbols. And Rank studied it as "the will to immortality," which meant to him man's inherent need to live in the light of eternity. Each of these terms involved a psychological experience, and each of them referred ultimately

---

*In fact, he tries to free these experiences from any supernatural connotations: "It is quite important to disassociate this experience from any theological or supernatural reference, *even though for thousands of years they have been linked*" (my italics!).[10]

to a contact with a larger realm of reality in which man's psychological nature transcends itself. Individually, Freud, Adler, Jung, and Rank came to this culminating insight, and the totality of their experiences form the foundations of the new psychology.[12]

This "new psychology" to which Progoff refers, is a psychology which takes with utmost seriousness the spiritual dimension of man. Psychologists of this ilk seek to learn more about man's capacity to experience God; to understand the dynamics of this experience; and to unlock ways that will free man for this experience. Carl Jung, in particular, has gleaned many valuable insights into the "other worldly" side of man; and more reference to his work will be made in subsequent chapters. For our purposes now, suffice it to say that Jung found in his practice of psychotherapy that when an individual finally confronted the "God-Archetype" which he says comprises the very core and foundation of the human personality, at that point his patient generally began to get well.

Consequently, when we speak about pilgrimage and do so in spiritual terms, we are not wandering off into any fanciful land. It is not only theology that speaks of man's growth in such terms. Now psychology is doing the same sort of thing. While this is a relatively new discovery for psychology, the Scriptures have been affirming man's spiritual nature for centuries. It is not without reason, therefore, that psychology is beginning to take such biblical insights very seriously.

▶ Inter Action

The New Psychology

There are many writers who seek to understand man's spiritual nature, individuals like Adler, Argyal, Frankl, Horney, Fromm, May, Rogers, Allport and of course Jung, Progoff, and Maslow. The following books, in addition to those already mentioned, might be of interest to those desiring to pursue further the ideas in this chapter.

1. *Encounter With God,* by Morton Kelsey (Minneapolis: Bethany Fellowship, Inc., 1972).
2. *Introduction to Jung's Psychology,* by Frieda Fordham (London: Penguin Books, 1953).
3. *Religion, Values, and Peak Experiences* by Abraham Maslow (New York: The Viking Press, 1964).
4. *The Kingdom Within,* by John A. Sanford (Philadelphia: J. B. Lippincott Co.).

Part II
The Geography
of Pilgrimage

These notes? They were sign-posts
erected after you had reached a
point where you needed them, a fixed
point which was on no account to be
lost sight of.

—Dag Hammarskjöld, *Markings*

4 Charting Our Pilgrimage

If it is true that each of us has a unique, God-given path to follow, it behooves us to discern that way and walk in it. Only then can we hope to fulfill our potential and be what God would have us be in this world. However, finding *our* path, *our* "calling," is not always easy. It is often difficult to sort through all the conflicting influences on our life to find that unique thing God wants of us. Yet we do have at least one very significant indicator to help us discern God's hand: our own past. Clues to our calling are often hidden in experiences we have had. Certain environments or situations may disclose aspects of our calling that we might otherwise miss or only discern much later on. It is important, therefore, to look carefully at our personal history. As we discern lines of growth and patterns of God's action in our life, we grow aware of who we are becoming, and in so doing know more clearly the way we ought to go in the future.

For the sake of providing a starting point for this sort of analysis, I have included the following chart. It will serve as a focal point for discussing patterns of pilgrimage and as a model for constructing a chart of our own. While it appears to indicate that the "model pilgrimage" consists of a steady movement from atheism to an encounter with Christian ideas followed by a conversion experience which in turn is followed by steady movement along the Christian path until one's death, this is *not* what I mean to imply by this chart. In fact, there really is no "ideal" or even "normal" pilgrimage. For example, a person may grow up in a Christian home and never know a time when he did not believe in Jesus. It is almost as if his whole life consisted of Phase III. Another individual may also start out in a Christian family but then violently reject Christianity and consciously move in the opposite direction for years before turning back to faith again. The shape of the line describing the direction of his pilgrimage would twist and turn in a much different pattern. The

38

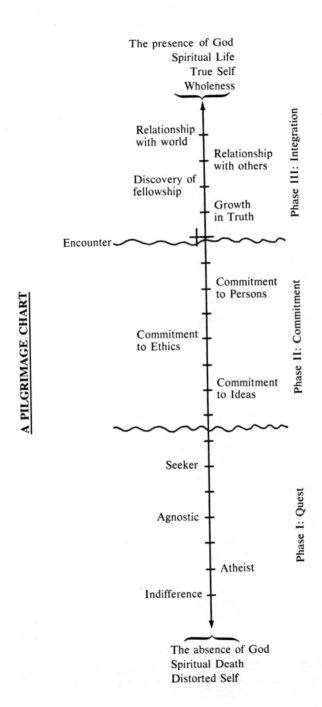

starting point, the intermediate stops, even the phases we go through, will be unique for each of us. So the chart is not a definition of the path everyone must tread, but a generalization of the experience, positions, and types of movement experienced by a great many people. As such, it has proved useful as the means whereby individuals have understood the meaning of their past life in such a way as to provide clues for what lies ahead. The past does contain the seeds of the future.

Perhaps the only element common to every chart is the two end points. Scripture is quite clear about this. Our life is either tending toward God or away from Him; there is no third alternative. Our pilgrimage can end in wholeness or in distortion. We can come to dwell in the presence of God or we can live in that place which is characterized by God's absence. The one pole, "the presence of God," "True Self," etc., is the goal of the pilgrim which we discussed in Chapter 2. The other outcome, "the absence of God," is more difficult to come to grips with. For one thing, this pole is defined in negatives. It consists of the *lack* of God's presence; of spiritual *death* or non-life; of Self that has been *distorted;* of Hell, if you like. It is hard to get a handle on that which is the negation of something quite concrete and real.

There is another difficulty. To speak about such a pole, one has to overcome the prevailing belief that no such negative outcome even exists! As C. S. Lewis notes, most of us share the view "that reality never presents us with an absolutely unavoidable 'either-or;' that, granted skill and patience and (above all) time enough, some way of embracing both alternatives can always be found; that mere development or adjustment or refinement will somehow turn evil into good without our being called on for a final and total rejection of anything we should like to retain."[1]

Unless we are of a vindictive nature, all of us want things "to work out for the best in the end" for everyone.[2] However, it is crystal clear that right here and now, each of us is tending in one of two quite opposite directions. We are either moving *toward God's presence,* albeit with fits, starts, and much hesitation; or we are moving *away from His presence* deliberately or simply by virtue of never having made up our minds to follow God. It is also clear that the one path leads to ever-increasing wholeness while the other brings distortions and imbalance to our personhood.

In other words, we *are* in the process of becoming what we choose. We really do have free will. Our choices count. And at death, our choice to seek God's presence or to flee from it will be confirmed. This is what I seek to express in the dual poles of the chart—that our life-tendency will have a real conclusion to it. We will find and dwell in the New Jerusalem, where God is and where, therefore, real reality exists; or we will be in that place where God is not; where nothing real exists; that place which is populated (if C. S. Lewis' speculation is right) by people who have shrunk down to nothing more than the greed, the lust, or the self-centeredness they nourished throughout their lives.

I think it is possible to see what I am saying about how our ongoing choices come to define our natures when one looks at the lives of old people in which the summation of choices is often clearer. I think of two older people I know. One woman, though in her eighties, is more alive, aware, and loving than most people fifty years her junior. She reads constantly and widely; is in touch with affairs around the world; prays for a wide range of people; gives of her meager income to a variety of charities; all the time patiently looking after another woman almost her own age who is failing in health. In a word, she is more whole than she has ever been, despite her age and infirmity. A host of tendencies and ongoing choices in her life are coming to fruition.

Another woman I know has shrunk. Her world, once fairly open, is now constricted basically to herself and her husband. She is bitter about a great deal. There are many people, even (or perhaps especially) those related to her, who have become, in her mind, "enemies." All her resources, financial and psychological, are channelled into the maintenance of her very private world. Looking back on her past life, it is possible to see how this happened. Her bitterness, her fear, her exclusiveness, were always there in some measure. But they grew in significance by virtue of the choices she kept on making until they began to dominate. Now she has given up trying to relate to the world around her, and this is all that is left. She has become what she kept on choosing. Incidentally, I expect both women will one day stand before Jesus. The faith of the second woman is quite genuine (as far as one can tell in such matters). However, she will have much to unlearn, whereas the first woman may well be like Sarah Smith of Golders Green in *The Great Divorce,* of whom little was known on earth but who in Heaven is attended by angels.

It also seems to be true that our pilgrimage goes through certain general phases. I have listed three: Quest, Commitment, and Integration. The first, Quest, is that period in our life during which we cast about for direction and try out different options. This is the time when we seek to find what is true; when we strive to discern that which is fundamentally "real" in the midst of a world in which much is mere illusion. At times this quest for direction is conscious and deliberate. All too often, however, we simply drift into a *weltanschauung* and generally, in the twentieth century at least, this means a purely naturalistic outlook. Certain people even make Quest into a life-style. They spend their time going from one exciting option to another—always seeking, never finding; never *willing* to find (or so it seems).

One thing is clear from Scripture. Man no longer lives in the direct relationship with God he once enjoyed. The fundamental goal of our Quest, then, is the recovery of the sense that we were made to know God and the discovery that we can be reconciled once again to our Creator. By virtue of Adam's choice, mankind decided to go it alone; to live in one world only (the natural), forsaking that other reality (the supernatural), for which he was also made. This is the meaning of the

Fall: man has become separated from God. As a result, no man automatically follows God's ways. We have to seek God in order to find Him. The Quest phase ends when we realize that in seeking truth we have been seeking Jesus who is Truth and who opens up the way back to God.

The Commitment phase covers that period of time during which we learn what would be involved if we were to live our life in relationship to Jesus Christ. For some people the span of time is very short between this discovery that Jesus can be known and their act of commitment to Him. But for others—and I think this is not always recognized—there is a longer period of time before they are able to give themselves to Jesus. Often this is a period of growing commitment characterized in turn by an acceptance of Jesus' teaching, an attempt to live by His principles, the joining of a fellowship which seeks to honor and worship Him and, finally, an encounter with the person of Jesus Himself.

Just as it is possible to stop before our Quest has led us to understand that God has revealed Himself in Jesus, so, too, it is possible to stop short of commitment to Jesus. There are not an inconsiderable number of individuals who would count themselves as Christians but whose commitment is solely to the *ideas* of Jesus. Theirs is a belief in dogma; a commitment to a certain theology. But commitment to ideas, no matter how accurate they may be, is ultimately a barren and sterile commitment. All we can do with an idea is believe it and then conform our life to it. After that, there is nothing more. Commitment to the Person who stands behind the ideas is quite a different stance, since commitment to a person is a growing, changing, deepening experience that develops as our life goes on. It is sad to realize how many of us have settled down at the point of Jesus' ideals, at the point of being a church member, or at the point of following His ethics, and never allowed the Commitment phase to bear its proper fruit which is allegiance to the Person of Jesus.

Many, however, do come to Jesus and ask Him to be their Lord. It is this encounter which marks the transition from the Commitment phase to the Integration phase. This final phase is characterized by an ongoing incorporation into our life of the insights and attitudes of Jesus, and by a widening understanding of the meaning and implications of our Christian faith. Our individual relationship to Jesus leads quite naturally to changes in our relationships with others, and eventually touches on our relationship to the world in general. This phase is open-ended, unlike the previous two which had definite culminating points. In fact, the integration of Christian truths and principles into our life really never ends until death. And who knows, perhaps after death we will go on learning and growing, unhampered by the fallen nature which so obstructed our previous growth.

It is possible, however, to become a settler at some point in this Integration phase, just as in any other. We have all met those individuals who are perennial "new Christians," who have taken only the first step on the Christian path, and then stopped. Others seem to discover a particular Christian truth, claim it as their own, and then never move beyond that one area of understanding. Still others, like the old woman I mentioned, stop without ever seeming to integrate their Christian beliefs into the rest of their life.

So it is clear that each pilgrimage is unique. Each person is at a different point, arrived at in his own special way. This is important to bear in mind. Since no two pilgrimages are alike, our only concern can be with our own path. What someone else's pilgrimage looks like is not our problem. C. S. Lewis illustrates this beautifully in his delightful children's story, *The Horse and His Boy*. At one point, the boy Shasta gets lost in a fog while riding in a forest. Aslan uses the occasion to correct the boy's false assessment of his pilgrimage.

> And as Shasta gaped with open mouth and said nothing, the Voice continued. "I was the lion who forced you to join with Aravis. I was the cat who comforted you among the houses of the dead. I was the lion who drove the jackals from you while you slept. I was the lion who gave the Horses the new strength of fear for the last mile so that you should reach King Lune in time. And I was the lion you do not remember who pushed the boat in which you lay, a child near death, so that it came to shore where a man sat, wakeful at midnight, to receive you."
> "Then it was you who wounded Aravis?"
> "It was I."
> "But what for?"
> "Child," said the Voice, "I am telling you your story, not hers. I tell no-one any story but his own."[3]

We get into trouble when we start comparing our path to that of someone else. "Why did he have it so easy," we ask and we are envious. Or we seek to model our pilgrimage after that of a person we admire and so we lose our own distinctiveness. Or we compare where we have arrived in our pilgrimage to the point at which another person is, and we feel superior (or depressed). None of these attitudes is healthy. Each story is unique. Each has its own inner logic. Each is in God's hand. In the end, our only concern is to follow faithfully the way God has marked out uniquely for us.

The really important thing is not *where* we are in our pilgrimage, but whether we are moving. Circumstance, temperament, opportunity, ability, and resources all affect the particular point at which we might be. I recall being involved in an evangelistic mission at a university in South Africa. At this particular mission we used a multi-media show as one means of presenting the Gospel. A student told me at one point during the mission that this multi-media show had affected him deeply. Prior to attending the show he had been an atheist, he said. After viewing it and then thinking about what had been presented, he decided he could no longer be an atheist. Now, he told me, he was an agnostic. At the time, I remember thinking that while I was glad for this change, still it was a pity that he had not actually become a Christian. Later it dawned on me just how significant this had been for the student. He had *moved*. Probably for the first time in his life there had been movement in his religious understanding. For him, at that time, this was all the movement that was possible. But he had moved, and who knows where that movement would take him. If he continued in this direction, he would eventually reach the place where he would be able to understand who Jesus is and then, one day, to commit himself to Him.

No matter where we are in our pilgrimage, God is there, too, accepting and loving us. Whether we are an atheist who is quite sure such an entity as "God" does not exist, a nominal church member with little real commitment, or a quiet and faithful follower of Jesus for thirty years, God loves each of us. And in each instance His Spirit is striving in our lives to open us to His Truth. God loves each one of us at each point in our lives.

I remember the first time I realized this. I was in Cape Town, participating in an evangelistic mission at the university. It was late in the evening and I was walking back to my room. It was one of those lush Cape Town nights: warm, quiet, the air filled with the fragrance of many flowers. I started thinking about some of the experiences I had had as a young Christian, some of the really dumb things I had done in my youthful sincerity. I was both amused and embarrassed as I realized how much I had really moved in my Christian life. Then the thought struck me. One thing had remained constant during all this time. I had had exactly the same sense of God's love for me when I was a very young Christian doing dumb things, as I had that moment in Cape Town. God loved me, not my so-called "spiritual maturity." He had loved me then as he loved me now. And in both instances His Spirit was at work gently seeking to move me on in my Christian life. It was also evident that one day I would look back at that moment in Cape Town and see just how inadequate my understanding, attitudes, and faith had been then. Our "spiritual maturity" is *never* all it could be, and to pretend that we are wise and mature is a sure sign of spiritual immaturity. Yet nevertheless, no matter whether we are experiencing success or failure, God is there, in His love, in His concern, in His acceptance. This is a fact to cherish.

▶ Inter Action

Charting

It is time now to begin constructing a personal pilgrimage chart. This is not a task, incidentally, which can be completed in a day. There are many dimensions that shape our personal pilgrimage, so we will be working on the various parameters of pilgrimage throughout the book.

It is time, too, to start dividing your notebook into sections. The easiest way to do this is to use index dividers in a standard three-ring notebook. This makes it possible to add to or to change your notebook as you grow in your use of it. At this point you need four categories:

1. *"Insights"*—a section in which you can record random thoughts or questions that strike you as you work through *Pilgrimage*.

2. *"Bible Studies"*—include in this section the Hebrews 11 study from Chapter Two.

3. *"Miscellaneous Exercises"*—put the "Pilgrim/Settler Quiz" here, as well as the "Pilgrim Images" exercise.

4. *"Pilgrimage Charts"*—You will use this section for the following exercise.

Spiritual Awareness Exercise

I. First of all, draw a chart that will express your own pilgrimage in terms of "spiritual awareness." By "spiritual awareness" I mean the degree to which you were conscious of God's reality and trying to live according to that awareness. Construct this chart by letting the vertical axis correspond to "Level of Spiritual Awareness" and the horizontal axis correspond to "Time."

In order to do this with some depth, I suggest that you first try to divide your life into various periods that were significant for you in terms of spiritual growth or lack of growth. These periods can be characterized by age (*e.g.*, "Early Times"); by place (*e.g.*, Minneapolis period"); by person (*e.g.*, a particular time span may be delineated for you by a key individual like your grandfather); by group (*e.g.*, "Young Life Phase"); by education (*e.g.*, "Graduate School"); or by the "position" you held or a philosophy that was key for you (*e.g.*, "Existentialist" phase). It will be interesting, when you are finished, to look at the *nature* of the influences in your past life. Have *people* generally been key for you; or do *groups* influence you a lot? This is a valuable insight into what type of influences are most conducive to your growth.

For each time period, note two things: 1.) The significant factors during that period (*e.g.*, an adult Sunday School class and C. S. Lewis books); and 2.) Any special events (*e.g.*, a deep, inner sense of God's overwhelming love for you that came one day during prayer).

Now, using this data, draw your chart, indicating your growth or diminishing level of spiritual awareness during each period. You may find that certain periods are so rich in growth that they demand separate charts covering just that period.

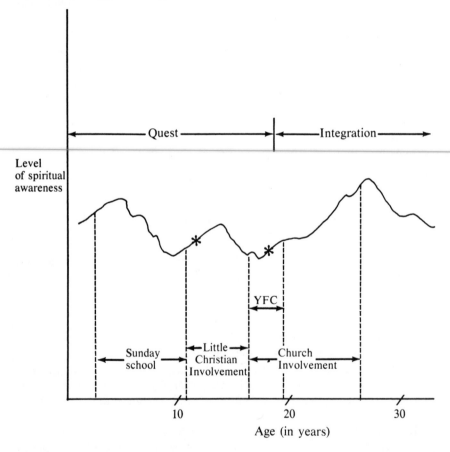

II. When your chart is finished:

A. Indicate on it, if possible, your Quest, Commitment, and Integrating phases.

B. Note with arrows the general direction of your life during each phase, i.e., whether you were moving toward God or away from Him.

C. Spend a few moments assessing where you are right now, in terms of spiritual awareness, especially in the light of your whole pilgrimage.

Example:

1. Childhood (to 11 years)

   a. Significant factors

      1. Awareness of God

      2. Mission Sunday School at the local school

      3. Daily Vacation Bible School in the tent

   b. Significant events

      1. At six, in my room, the sense that God wanted me to "speak for Him."

      2. Eleven years—"giving my heart to Jesus" at Sunday School.

2. Early Teens (12 to 15)

   a. Significant factors

      1. Away every weekend, little Christian involvement.

      2. Freshman year in high school and sense that I should be involved in Christian activities.

   b. Significant events

      Coming home late after parties and being aware of my loneliness.

5 Quest

The Quest phase of pilgrimage is that period of time during which an individual seeks to discover whether God does in fact exist and if He can be known. It is a time when basic questions are asked concerning the nature of reality and the meaning of truth. It is the period in life when a person develops his inquisitive faculties as a result of his search for a truth that is sufficient to build a life upon.

The whole subject of the quest for truth is a large and complicated one, touching upon philosophy, psychology, the history of ideas and many other areas. My aim in this chapter is not to try to treat it in all of its wide-ranging implications, but to discuss the quest for truth *as it relates to Christian pilgrimage: i.e.,* I will focus on those steps whereby a person comes to the point that he is willing and able to give himself to God through Jesus Christ. For some, this search is long and arduous. For others, it seems to take no time at all. Still others never even have to search at all. They know Jesus from their youth. How long the Quest phase takes is not the important thing, however. That one eventually does arrive at an understanding of God's self-revelation in Jesus is what really counts.

It is quite obvious that there are different viewpoints when it comes to the question of God. Some people believe in God, others wonder if He exists, still others are certain that He does not. Among those who believe in a God, there are different understandings of His nature. Is He personal and hence knowable? Or is "God" just another name for an abstract Life-Force which swirls blindly through the universe? On the chart I have indicated various points of view about God. These do not indicate *all* the possible attitudes, but I think that they are representative of most of the ways people think about God. We all start out holding one of these viewpoints. Perhaps we adopt our parent's perspective, or maybe we have been influenced by a particular teacher at school or by

QUEST

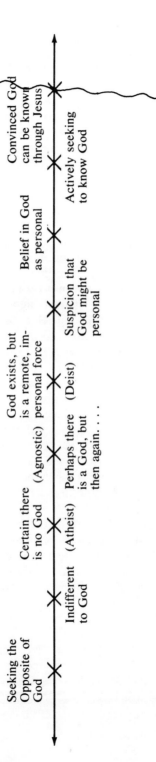

Seeking the Opposite of God

Indifferent to God

Certain there is no God (Atheist)

Perhaps there is a God, but then again. . . . (Agnostic)

God exists, but is a remote, impersonal force (Deist)

Suspicion that God might be personal

Belief in God as personal

Actively seeking to know God

Convinced God can be known through Jesus

our peers in general. Regardless of the source, this perspective forms the starting point for our personal pilgrimage.

Rather than beginning this discussion of specific positions by starting at one end of the chart or the other, I want to begin in the middle with the points labeled "atheist" and "agnostic." These are, perhaps, the most familiar categories when speaking of disbelief in Christianity. An atheist is a person who denies that there is a God. An agnostic does not go quite that far. While he feels that God probably does not exist, he is uncertain enough to leave open the option that He might. It is fairly difficult to find a really authentic atheist anymore. The problem is that it takes far too much certainty to hold such a position and ours is an age characterized by doubt. To be an atheist you must really have thought about the issues and come to some firm conclusions. The atheist has studied. He has weighed the pros and cons. He has reason for this viewpoint.

Agnosticism, on the other hand, is a much easier position to hold. God may exist, the agnostic says, but then again, He may not. Intellectually, it is all very open-minded, but in practice the agnostic lives as if God did not exist. Needless to say, at times agnosticism is simply an excuse for not doing much serious thinking. But, to be fair, this is not always the case. Many agnostics have arrived at their position as a result of much search. They would like to believe in God, but, as of yet, they are not able to do so in all integrity.

The deist* goes a step beyond the agnostic. He believes in a god. However, the god of the deist is not the God of the New Testament, *i.e.,* an active, personal Being who loves and can be loved. The deist's god is impersonal, generally very remote and probably better conceived of as an abstract force than as a living Being. There are a great many people today who qualify as deists, even though most of them would be surprised to find out that this is what they are. You see, a man's god, his real god, as Paul Tillich and others have pointed out, is that which shapes his day-to-day decisions. And I am labeling as a deist anyone whose choices are motivated by one of the many impersonal forces to which twentieth century man gives his allegiance. I have in mind such things as "the desire for wealth," the "need for security," the "craving for power," or even "love of one's family." All of these can and have become "gods" when commitment to them gets out of hand and they begin to dominate a life. For example, a man may work late each night, go into the office on weekends, espouse only those ideas currently acceptable in his firm, attempt to reshape his wife and family into the company image, and never say "No" to any request his boss might make. In so doing, his "desire to succeed" has become his *de facto* god.

---

*Properly speaking, "deist" is an historical term used to describe 18th Century rationalists who believed in God as a creative force but rejected religion. I am using the term in the broader sense of anyone who believes in a non-personal God.

When a choice has to be made (*e.g.,* between taking his son fishing or picking up his boss's nephew at the airport) the will of his god prevails (he drives to the airport).

Such gods can be very powerful because they are seldom recognized for what they really are. In fact, a man can be an active church member (or a vocal atheist, for that matter) while at the same time actually giving his allegiance to one of these impersonal gods. There are probably many more actual deists than there are people who even know what the word means!

There are convenient labels for the three positions I have discussed so far, and there are a great many people who hold such points of view. There are no such one-word definitions to describe the positions at either extreme on my chart. The reason is, I think, that there are far fewer people to be found holding these perspectives.

Located on the right side of the chart are those positions held by people who are tending toward belief. Such individuals have moved from a comfortable uncertainty to an uncomfortable wondering. For them, the question: "Does God really exist?" is no longer a topic for idle speculation. It is an issue that demands an answer. But, even though such people have come a long way toward belief, their Quest is not yet over, and the answers they seek are not always easily available. For one thing, prejudice stands in the way. It is increasingly thought naive and unmodern to be a Christian. Christianity demands too much certainty, too much commitment, to fit in with today's ethos in which all values and all traditional ways of thinking are suspect. There is also misunderstanding. As John Baille has noted in commenting on his discussions with non-believing friends: "It is seldom, if ever, that I have felt their doubts and denials to be based upon a true comprehension of what they were doubting and denying . . . It is extraordinary how widely the modern world has forgotten what Christianity really is."[1] Yet in the end, all this does not matter to the person who has caught a glimpse of eternity. He simply must know if God is real and so he presses on through the misunderstanding and through the prejudice until he finds the answers he needs. As Jesus Himself said, if we will but seek, we will find (Matt. 7:7).

Perhaps it is useful to think of the various categories on the right side of the chart as positions of increasing fluidity. If so, the categories on the left are quite different. They indicate positions of increasing rigidity. They also indicate positions of increasing distance from God. The first step beyond atheism is indifference. Here the question of God no longer really matters. An indifferent person does not care enough even to argue that God does not exist. It is a position of no belief. This is why I have located "indifference" to the left of atheism, which is still a type of belief. An atheist believes God does not exist, and is prepared to defend his views. As such, he is open to reason and to experience. It is not inconceivable that he may change his mind and become a Christian. This is seldom the case with the really indifferent person. He simply does not care.

Indifference seems to develop in a person. I do not believe it is natural in anyone, for the innate tendency in mankind is to wonder and to question. Yet this questing spirit can be killed off. How it happens is unclear. Perhaps it is due to satiation, that boredom which sets in when a person has so much of everything that he can find nothing new. Yet this is not the whole story. Satiation can lead to search, as more than one converted rock-star has testified. Whatever the cause, indifference is a much deadlier enemy than atheism. It is almost impossible to combat the "I really don't care" attitude in ourselves.

There is at least one other position on the unbelief side of the chart: the active seeking after evil. In cases of extreme indifference, a person may become so bored that he turns to the perverse to see if perhaps a spark of excitement might be found. However, this is not the only path by which a spiritual quest turns from Light to Darkness wherein the Prince of This World is sought in all his destructiveness. Let there be no mistake. Not all the forces we encounter in our pilgrimage are of man's creation. And there are those among us who have *chosen* to follow what God is not. The results of that choice are devastatingly portrayed by Charles Williams in his novel, *War in Heaven:*

> This was no longer mission or desire, search or propaganda or hunger; this was rejection absolute. No mortal mind could conceive a desire which was not based on a natural and right desire; even the hunger for death was but a perversion of the death which precedes all holy birth. But of every conceivable and inconceivable desire this was the negation. This was desire itself sick, but not unto death; rejection which tore all things asunder and swept them with it in its fall through the abyss.[2]

The positions indicated on our chart are indeed real positions, not theoretical abstractions. But while we have isolated them for purposes of discussion, it ought to be pointed out that these labels are not absolute. Real people quite often hold mixtures of various positions. For example, a person might honestly call himself an agnostic although he is quite indifferent to the whole question of God. Yet another *bonafide* agnostic might be actively seeking to know if there is a God. Their labels are identical, yet their attitudes are quite different. In fact, our attitude at any given position is at least as important as that position itself. The attitude that leads to growth is characterized by an active commitment to searching out what is true, using one's position as a basis for this search.

We should also remember that labels are not meant to be used as a means of judgment. They are really only useful when applied to ourselves in order to understand where *we* are, so as to know what lines of inquiry we need to undertake in order to grow. Labels are also useful to us personally when they serve as bench marks by which we can plot our personal movement and growth. This, after all, is the really essential thing; not where we might be at a given point in time, but the direction in which we are moving. With this in mind, let us turn our attention to the really crucial problem for the pilgrim: how to move from one of these positions to another.

In general terms there are two issues which have to be resolved before any movement can take place: the issues of need and belief. No one will make any move unless he feels it is important to move. Nor will he move unless he believes he is going to a position of truth. We hold to our viewpoints very tenaciously. After all, our position is *our* position. We have a stake in it. It expresses who we are. We have defended it in the past and will do so in the future—*unless* we are convinced that it is invalid or inadequate (*i.e.*, our belief about what is true has changed) and that it is vital for us to move to a new viewpoint (*i.e.*, we sense our need to change).

In terms of belief, there is really only one issue to be settled before we are able to come to Christian commitment: what do we think of Jesus Christ? If we are able to affirm that He is the Son of God through whose death and resurrection reconciliation to God is made possible, then this settles the question of belief for us at this point in our pilgrimage. However, for many people, there is a long road ahead before they reach the place where they can ever face this issue, much less resolve it. Various obstacles have to be overcome first. For some, it is philosophical problems which provide a stumbling block to their acceptance of Christianity. For others, it is existential issues which are the hindrance. They wonder, for example, if Christianity really does bring meaning to life. Still others stumble over specific questions, *e.g.*, "If God is all good, how can there be evil in the universe?" Some people have problems as a result of a commitment to the tenets of a specific discipline like psychology. A behaviorist, for example, will ask: "Is man anything more than a complex set of conditioned responses?" Some even set up Christianity in opposition to science in general and need to see that this is a fictitious dichotomy.

No matter what the issue, it has got to be faced and cleared up. Obviously this is not the place to try to examine in detail all the potential stumbling blocks. These are problems that demand serious and lengthy interaction. There are, however, ample books that do just this. These are not, after all, new questions. Christians down through the ages have had to face these same issues, so there is no lack of interactive material. I have listed some of it in the bibliography at the end of the Inter Action section.

Let me add one proviso to what I have just said. There is a way around the often long and tedious study required to make sense out of some of these knotty problems. This is the route of experience. At times, God in His grace short-circuits our problems by directly confronting us with His Presence and in so doing settles issues in a way no chain of argument could ever hope to do. But while this may happen to some, others will come to Him via the more difficult route of slow, methodical probing of the issues until they clearly see Who He is. If this is our lot we can be sure that in the economy of the Kingdom there is a purpose in the process. Perhaps it is necessary in terms of our calling to have thought through the issues in depth.

Once we have cleared away the tangle of issues that obscure our vision and have come to see that Christianity may indeed be true, we have arrived at the point where we must consider who Jesus is. This is the heart of the issue. But how can we know who Jesus is? Aren't we dependent upon *a priori* belief in the Bible since this is the major source of information about Jesus? It seems that in order to find faith one must already have faith. To be sure the Bible declares that faith is a gift from God. It is the Holy Spirit who opens our eyes so that we can "see" what Christianity is all about. However, this is not to say that we have to depend solely on some sort of spiritual intuition in order to know that Jesus is God incarnate. After all, Christianity is a religion rooted in history. Jesus was a historical figure. He died a real death and experienced a literal resurrection. And because this is so, all of these issues can be investigated *by use of the historical method*.

Since this is such a crucial issue, I want to outline the way in which a person can come to understand who Jesus is by means of history alone. This particular approach is not dependent on *a priori* faith in the Bible, but requires that we use the same methods historians use daily when they probe any historical problem. We can do so by asking five basic questions:

1. Do we have documents which give us reliable information about Jesus?

2. If we do have accurate information about Jesus, who did He claim to be?

3. If Jesus claimed to be God, does the evidence indicate that He was joking, lying, mad or telling the truth?

4. Was His life consonant with the claim to be God or in contradiction to it?

5. Since His resurrection from the dead is the ultimate fact supporting His claim to be God, does the evidence verify His resurrection?

Needless to say, I have personally concluded that the weight of the evidence indicates that Jesus was (and is) exactly who He claimed to be—God incarnate. Those who wish to pursue the discussion in full should refer to the books listed in this chapter's bibliography, especially John Stott's *Basic Christianity* and John Montgomery's *History and Christianity*.

Yet even this sort of inquiry is not sufficient in and of itself. You see, it is possible to come to believe that Jesus is God and still not be a

Christian. There was a good example of this during a university mission in which I participated. At one point I gave a lecture in which I presented the historical evidence for Jesus' resurrection. One of the student interns who was working with us brought two friends to this particular meeting. Afterwards he asked them what they thought about the lecture.

"A very impressive case," one of the students replied. "I had no idea there was so much historical proof that Jesus rose from the dead." The other student concurred in this opinion.

The conversation continued until both students admitted that they now felt Christianity was probably true. At this point, my friend asked the obvious question: "Well, does this mean you are going to become Christians?"

They were a bit taken back by this question.

"No," they replied, "probably not." They explained that while the idea of the resurrection was an intriguing one, in fact, they personally were not really all that interested in Christianity.

Here was a perfect example of belief without commitment. Just because a person believes certain historical facts, this does not necessarily mean that he will change his life because of these intellectual convictions. A historian may believe as a result of his study that capitalism is in danger of imminent disaster, yet this does not necessarily mean he will run out and sell all his stocks and bonds and move to a socialist country. As the old saying goes: You can lead a horse to water but you can't make him drink. The same is true when it comes to Christian commitment. You can argue a man into submission until he has no choice but to believe (or admit he is a fool), but you cannot force him to open his life joyously to this same Jesus you have persuaded him is the Son of God. Commitment is still a personal matter—and well it should be, or we would all be under the sway of one demigod or another.

Hence it is obvious that there is a second vital aspect which underlies all movement during the Quest phase: the inner desire to change. It is a sense of need that turns belief into commitment. But what are the roots of this desire to change? They vary from person to person. Perhaps for us a sense of dissatisfaction is the root cause which creates a need to change. We have seen through the ideology that we held for so long. We sense we must move our lives onto a firmer footing by commiting ourselves to a perspective that is more in touch with reality. This is intellectual dissatisfaction. Moral or spiritual dissatisfaction is an even stronger driving force. We come to see deep inadequacies in our lives. Perhaps a relationship sours that we took for granted and we are startled to find it was our insensitivities that ruined it. Or perhaps tragedy of one sort or another overtakes us and we discover that when the props are knocked away, we really *can't* cope. Whatever the cause, the result is dissatisfaction with the *status quo* and a deep desire to change.

Or the whole thing may be more a matter of longing than it is of dissatisfaction. Things are going well, but yet we *know* there ought to be more to life. Perhaps we have caught glimpses from time to time of another, more fulfilling way to live and it is our longing to be part of that way of life that creates within us this need to change.

Our need may be generated simply by the desire to become more whole. We realize our inadequacies. We want to grow into a more creative, a more giving person. So we are open to whatever will promote this wholeness we desire.

Perhaps the strongest motivation to change comes as a result of a numinous experience of the sort mentioned in Chapter Three (which will be touched on in more detail in Chapter Seven). Different people describe these experiences in different ways, but generally everyone agrees that out of them one gets a new perspective on the nature of the world. During such an experience it is as if one were lifted out of the ordinary world of sight, sound, and touch and given a glimpse of what lies behind what we call "reality." It is not uncommon to feel bitter disappointment upon return to the "normal" world.

Consider an experience of Carl Jung's that occurred in 1944, while he was recovering from an illness. Jung saw visions—the earth, from far out in space; a huge stone, the size of a meteorite; a temple containing an illuminated room, in which he was to learn the truth about his life. Finally he saw his own doctor, Dr. H. In Jung's own words:

> I knew at once: "Aha, this is my doctor, of course, the one who has been treating me. But now he is coming in his primal form. . . ."
>
> As he stood before me, a mute exchange of thought took place between us. Dr. H. had been delegated by the earth to deliver a message to me, to tell me that there was a protest against my going away. I had no right to leave the earth and must return. The moment I heard that, the vision ceased.
>
> I was profoundly disappointed, for now it all seemed to have been for nothing. . . . I was not allowed to enter the temple, to join the people in whose company I belonged.
>
> . . . .
>
> I felt a violent resistance to my doctor because he had brought me back to life. At the same time, I was worried about him. "His life is in danger, for heaven's sake! He has appeared to me in his primal form! When anybody attains this form it means he is going to die, for already he belongs to the 'greater company.' "
>
> In actual fact I was his last patient. On April 4, 1944—I still remember the exact date—I was allowed to sit up on the edge of my bed for the first time since the beginning of my illness, and on this same day Dr. H. took to his bed and did not leave it again. . . . Soon afterward he died of septicemia.
>
> Although my belief in the world returned to me, I have never since entirely freed myself of the impression that this life is a segment of existence which is enacted in a three-dimensional boxlike universe especially set up for it.

I would never have imagined that any such experience was possible. It was not a product of imagination. The visions and experiences were utterly real; there was nothing subjective about them; they all had a quality of absolute objectivity.

After the illness a fruitful period of work began for me. A good many of my principal works were written only then. The insight I had had, or the vision of the end of all things, gave me the courage to undertake new formulations. I no longer attempted to put across my own opinion, but surrendered myself to the current of my thoughts. Thus one problem after the other revealed itself to me and took shape.[3]

In each of these ways we are brought to the point where we want to change. Then what we have come to believe in a theoretical way becomes important to us in terms of our life, because these beliefs now serve to point out the direction in which we ought to change. When belief and need come together we are ready to move into the next phase of our pilgrimage: Commitment.

While the Quest phase of pilgrimage has a definite conclusion to it (*i.e.,* you come to the point where you want to encounter Jesus), the basic *attitude* which characterizes this phase ought to carry over to the whole of the pilgrimage. This is, of course, the attitude of inquiry; *i.e.,* the willingness to go on examining one's beliefs. In other words, the search for truth does not end with the discovery that Jesus is Lord of the Universe. In fact, it only really begins at that point. Now the focus shifts to the ongoing discovery of the wide-ranging implications of this foundational truth. This same attitude of critical inquiry which leads us to Jesus will go on unlocking new understandings and new depths throughout our life. Inquiry is, after all, a characteristic of the pilgrim. Resting upon what you have found is the attitude of the settler.

Before we lay aside the Quest phase of pilgrimage, one further comment is in order. Many Christians have not ever gone through a Quest phase as I have discussed it. They never really had to move from unbelief to belief; or if they did, it happened without much agony or searching. This was certainly my own experience. I always believed in God. I was exposed from childhood to various types of Christian input which I quite easily accepted until finally in high school, as a result of the influence of the Youth For Christ Club, I made a firm decision to follow Jesus. My own Quest phase came much later, after I had completed college and seminary, and when I began work in university ministries. Then I was exposed to the sorts of questions I have been discussing in this chapter. Only then did I begin to examine seriously the foundations of my faith.

No matter when it comes, this is an important process for each Christian. It is vital to know that what we believe is not based on some first-century fairy tale. In other words, Quest is not really an option for the Christian. During some period in his Christian life he has got to take it upon himself to investigate the foundations of his faith. This is a vital and necessary aspect of each pilgrimage.

▶ Inter Action

Seeking Truth

I. Quest Chart

It is time to focus your thoughts on your own Quest, be it past or present, with the aim of charting this period of your life. There are several ways of approaching this, depending upon the particular nature of your own experience.

A. From doubt to faith

If you did move from unbelief to belief in the manner discussed in this chapter:

1. Recall and note each step along the way, identifying each point with a label, if one exists, or a phrase that describes how you felt about God.

2. What was the nature of your doubt at each point? What were the questions you had to face?

3. What freed you to move on at each step of the way? Try to pin-point the nature of the influences which led to your growth. Was it a significant person? A friend? An authority figure? A book? A lecture? A sudden insight?

4. Translate all this into a chart, with "Belief in God" as the vertical axis and "Time" as the horizontal.

Example of Quest Chart*

a. "Comfortable Agnosticism" (1950 to 1971)
—our family never was very 'religious' except for one uncle who was a bit of a nut.
—I played baseball on a church team because they needed a catcher and I guess I "believed in God" because everyone else did but I forgot all about this when the season was over (1963).
—once in high school, a teacher discussed world religions. I was worried for a while that I didn't have any real religion (1965).

---

*Unlike many of the previous examples, this is not my own experience which is referred to here.

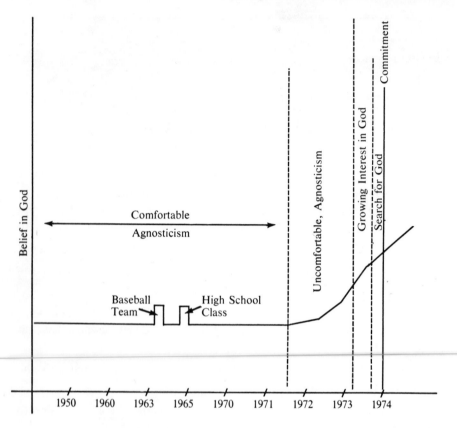

b. "Uncomfortable Agnosticism" (1971-72)
—my senior year in college I got to be good friends with a girl in my major and through her I met a lot of her friends, all of whom seemed to be Christians (she was too). We argued a lot. For the first time, I had to defend the fact that I did not believe in God. I didn't do too well, but never admitted I had any doubt I was right. What troubled me was:

1) I found intelligent, likeable people who actually believed in God.

2) This belief was very important to them—central in fact to their outlook

3) I saw there were good arguments for the existence of God. I especially could not get around why it is that men from every culture have a sense of right and wrong—which didn't seem possible if the universe was meaningless and neutral.

4) My pride kept me from admitting I could be wrong.

c. "Growing Interest in God" (1972-73)
—I took a job in a new city and didn't know many people. I

was lonely and often remembered the good times during senior year and the discussions we had about God.

—I stopped by the church down the street out of boredom (loneliness?) one Sunday, liked the minister and so began attending (March 1973).

—Got involved in a singles group at the church.

   d. "Search for God" (1973-)

—went to singles retreat for a weekend and came away with a deep desire to find out if God existed. I had been especially moved by the new insight that God might really *love* me. Had to know if this was so.

—Read a lot

—Saw the senior pastor several times

   e. "Commitment" (In 1974)

—alone in my room after the Christmas Eve service I opened my life to this God who loved me so much He sent His Son into this world.

B. From Awareness to Faith

Doubt is not a factor for some people. Their experience is one of simply growing in knowledge and understanding of God until they finally realize their need to open up to Him on a personal level. If this is your situation, draw a chart which will reflect your growing awareness of God over a period of time, noting at each stage the major influences upon you.

II. Facing the Issues: A Bibliography

There are many issues which must be faced before a person can come to faith in Christ. Some of these issues are peripheral in that while they cloud the situation, resolving them does not lead·to faith. Their resolution does, however, make it possible for the central issue of who Jesus is to be faced. The following is a brief listing of books which might prove useful in pursuing some of these issues. The list is by no means complete (*e.g.,* none of these treat issues on a specialist level). However, these are books which have proved useful to people in their Quest. They in turn will make references to other books which can be consulted if you wish to look into a particular subject in more detail.

Before you consult this bibliography, however:

List those questions which really trouble you (*e.g.,* "How can I integrate insights from eastern religions into an understanding of Christianity?"). Look through the list for an appropriate book which might shed some light on the question (*e.g., Christianity and Comparative Religions*).

Think about whether you really do understand the historical argument for the deity of Jesus. If not, plan on getting either *Basic Christianity* or *History and Christianity*.

If you do understand this line of argument, is there one link in the chain of reasoning at which your understanding is vague (*e.g.*, the fact that the New Testament is historically reliable)? *Choose* a book which addresses this issue (*e.g.*, *Are the New Testament Documents Reliable?*)

A. General Issues

1. General Questions

a. *Know Why You Believe,* by Paul Little (Scripture Press, Inc.)
b. *Reasons for Faith,* by Oliver Barclay (IV Press)

2. World Views: The following authors interact with various life perspectives ranging from eastern religion to the implications of Hegelian thought-patterns.

a. *The Dust of Death,* by Os Guinnes (IV Press)
b. *The God Who Is There* by Francis Schaeffer (IV Press)
c. *The Universe Next Door,* by James Sire (IV Press)—a catalogue of modern world views
d. *Christianity and Comparative Religions,* by J. N. .D Anderson (Tyndale Press)
e. *Christ and the Modern Mind,* edited by Robert Smith (IV Press)—26 essays interacting with different academic disciplines and their particular perspective

3. Theological Issues

a. *Miracles,* by C. S. Lewis (Macmillian)
b. *The Problem of Pain,* by C. S. Lewis (Macmillian)

4. Science

a. *Christianity in a Mechanistic Universe,* edited by D. M. Mackay (IV Press)
b. *Science and Christian Belief,* by C. A. Coulson (Fontana)

5. Christianity as a Way of Life

a. *The Abolition of Man,* by C. S. Lewis (Collier Books)—a brilliant discussion of man's innate sense of right and wrong
b. *A Song of Ascents,* by E. Stanley Jones (Abingdon)
c. *The Meaning of Persons; Guilt and Grace;* and *Escape From Loneliness* by Paul Tournier
d. *Surprised by Joy* by C. S. Lewis (Macmillan)

B. Who is Jesus?

1. Trustworthiness of the Documents

a. *Are the New Testament Documents Reliable?* by F. F. Bruce (IV Press)

b. *The Ring of Truth,* by J. B. Phillips

2. The Person of Jesus

a. *Basic Christianity* by John Stott (IV Press)
b. *Jesus and His Story,* by Ethelbert Stauffer (Alfred Knopf)—
historical evidence about Jesus from non-biblical sources

3. The Resurrection

a. *Man Alive,* by Michael Green (IV Press)
b. *The Davidson Affair,* by Stuart Jackman (Faber)

4. The Case for Christianity

a. *Basic Christianity,* by John Stott (IV Press)—an extremely
lucid presentation, an excellent place to begin
b. *Mere Christianity,* by C. S. Lewis (Macmillan)
c. *History and Christianity* by John Montgomery (IV Press)—a
summary of the basic historical argument

6 Commitment

I recall several people from my past. The first is a man I knew in high school. All the kids knew him. He was the head of a large Christian youth organization, which he held together because he was a tireless organizer and an unparalleled fund raiser. All his energy went into the promotion and expansion of this work. A few years after I left high school, I heard that he was no longer involved with the group. He had to resign his post as a result of some sort of sexual scandal. There was also talk of financial irregularities.

Then there are the various British expatriates I met while working in Africa. These men and women were individuals of impeccable character. They were honest, loyal, hard-working, and humble—a direct reflection of their Church-of-England upbringing. They were not at all interested, however, in Christian ideas, much less Christian doctrine. They simply lived, almost by reflex, in accord with Christian ethics.

I also remember a Christian businessman, a member of the Gideons, a pillar of his church. He was known for his aggressive personal witness. He constantly sought to share the truth of Christianity with others. However, when it came to business, it was every man for himself. There was not a little anger directed at him for what was thought to be his disregard for the needs and rights of others when he was involved with them in business transactions.

Then there is the woman in Johannesburg who tirelessly worked for the rights of the African people because, she said, this was our responsibility as Christians. Yet when she and my wife were talking on one occasion, the name of Jesus came up in the course of conversation. "You can't imagine how hard it is for me to respond positively to that name," this woman said. "Because of my background I associate Jesus with repression of black people, narrow-mindedness, and joylessness."

The final individual is the pastor of a small church. He had been in the ministry for years. I met him at a Billy Graham Rally. He told me that at a similar meeting a few nights previously he had committed his life to Christ for the first time.

What do all these individuals have in common? Obviously they are all involved with Christianity in one way or another. In fact, they each share a fair degree of commitment as is evidenced by their life and activities. *But the specific nature of each person's commitment is quite different,* and this is what interests me.

The first man was committed to a Christian organization. He did not share an equal commitment, so it seems, to Christian ethics. The second group of people, the British civil servants, were committed to Christian ethical standards. They were not, however, committed to Christian doctrine. The Christian businessman *was* committed to the doctrines of Christianity. This was "truth" for him. Yet, if his business dealings were any indication, his commitment did not extend to people. The woman in Johannesburg was most certainly committed to people. She was not committed to Jesus, however. Finally, there is the pastor who was personally committed to Christianity in every way but one. He held Christian ideas, lived by Christian ethics, worked in a Christian church, and served people as a Christian minister. He had not, however, been committed to Jesus.

The point should be obvious by now. *There are various levels of Christian commitment.* It may be necessary for a person to progress through stages of commitment just as he went from point to point during the Quest phase. He may, for example, begin by being committed to Christian doctrine and ethics, then move to a commitment to the church, and out of this develop a commitment to people in general until finally he becomes aware of his need to give his life to Jesus.

A different person may by-pass all this, and go directly from the discovery that Christianity is true to commitment to Jesus. This does not mean that such a person can neglect commitment in these other areas. His commitment to Christian ideas and ethics, and to Christian community and service to others, will have to come in the context of his Christian growth, *i.e.,* during the Integration Phase.

No matter how the process takes place, *Christian pilgrimage demands commitment in at least five areas*. There is commitment to Christian ideas, to Christian ethics, to the Christian community, to people in general, and to Jesus as a Person. If there is a lack of commitment in any one of these broad areas, this could well be the obstacle that is stymieing further Christian growth. It will be useful, therefore, to examine each of these different areas of commitment.

Before doing so, however, we need to discuss *non-commitment,* because it provides a useful foil against which to analyze commitment itself.

Non-commitment is a very popular option in this day and age. J. B. Phillips calls it "cozy agnosticism" and has some valuable insights into its nature.

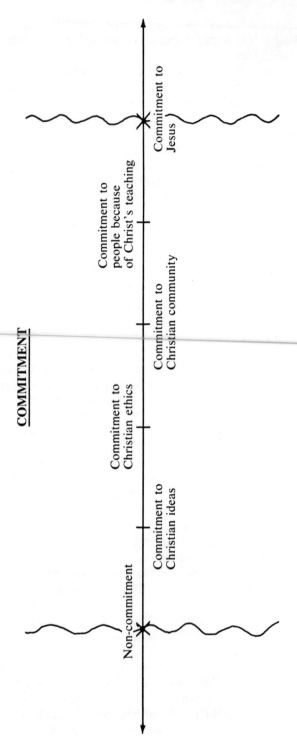

COMMITMENT

Non-commitment

Commitment to Christian ideas

Commitment to Christian ethics

Commitment to Christian community

Commitment to people because of Christ's teaching

Commitment to Jesus

So long as a man can persuade himself that he may honestly maintain an open mind about the identity and person of Jesus Christ, he remains uncommitted to the real business of living. Since he has no real standards he can be tolerant in isolation instead of becoming embarrassingly involved. Since he is unenlisted in any supra-human purpose, he is free to give or withhold himself as he chooses. Since he owes loyalty to nothing but his own humanist ideals, he is under no personal obligation to touch or to be touched by the evil he deplores. And since he is responsible to no one, he need feel no particular guilt or failure in avoiding battles in which he can observe a pitiful minority struggling ineffectually. This attitude of non-committal detachment is one of the most crippling evils of our time.[1]

Non-commitment carries with it real dangers. Viewed on a societal level, we can see that if the citizens of a democracy are not committed to the ideals of that society, in due time it will fail. Viewed on a personal level, it is clear that if individuals are not committed to the welfare of others, relationships will break apart—be they marriages, communes, or friendships. On an individual level, commitment is vital in order to coalesce the forces of the self into a directed whole. Psychologist W. Curry Mavis writes:

Commitment enlists all the dynamics of the personality in an effort to achieve a desired objective. It awakens dormant interest. It challenges lethargic talents. It enlists the energies and organizes them in effective effort. It rallies the scattered forces of personality and unites them in a drive to accomplish that which is of supreme personal importance. It concentrates faith on a system of integrated concerns and thus does away with a useless dissipation of energy.[2]

Commitment is vital for the pilgrim. Without it there will never be a focus to his life, much less sustained movement toward his desired goal.

The first step beyond non-commitment is usually "commitment to ideas." A person comes to believe that Christian doctrine is true and commits himself to the Christian position. This is well and good. Indeed, the Christian viewpoint on the nature of reality is accurate. But there is a problem when one's Christian commitment stops with doctrine, and unfortunately it is shared by numerous individuals. For them, Christianity *is* doctrine. It is doctrine they study, doctrine they defend, and doctrine which they use to put up walls between themselves and others. Such people are not really interested in ethics except as another species of Christian idea. Their alignment with a Christian body is motivated more by a desire to "learn about Christianity" than it is to be a part of a supporting, giving fellowship. When it comes to Jesus, their commitment to Him is as a great teacher.

But commitment to ideas alone can be deadly. Ideas are often cold, precise assertions which leave no room for the messy realities of life itself. A person who is fanatically committed to an idea (no matter how grand or true that idea may be) has the potential to disrupt and destroy all manner of relationships. To be in the grip of an idea can be a fearful thing, unless this commitment is balanced by other commitments, such as to people. Furthermore, doctrine is non-personal, and has no power in itself. While an idea can change our lives by drawing us into conformity with it, in and of itself it has no power to effect that change. This is why it is necessary to move beyond ideas to Jesus, the author of what we say we believe. He alone has the power to bring about on-going change in our lives.

Commitment to ethics is not unlike commitment to ideas since an ethic is a type of idea. But since it is a statement which relates to how we ought to live and behave in the company of others, it is a step forward from commitment to abstract theology. For example, there is a difference between commitment to the idea that baptism is a Christian obligation and commitment to the ethical statement: "Put away falsehood and let everyone speak the truth" (Eph. 4:25). This first commitment has little to do with human relationships. The second, a commitment to the honesty principle, has everything to do with how one relates to others. To be committed to Christian ethics is to be committed to a definite pattern of behavior toward other people.

But again, commitment to Christian ethics without the balancing effect of other commitments, has its problems. It is not unknown for very moral individuals to be censorious and aloof from "lesser mortals." The problem is that such people refuse to temper their ethical stance by a similar commitment to things such as mercy, forgiveness, and love, which are also biblical. Consequently, it can be quite "right" to turn out of your house an unwed but pregnant daughter. After all, sex before marriage is not allowed, and to lower standards, it is felt, is to belittle ethical commitment.

Clearly, then, commitment to ethical ideas is inadequate in and of itself. An ethic is a hard-and-fast statement about human behavior. It often does not take into account individual situations. Suppose, for example, that a man is an habitual liar. Now he may know that lying is ethically wrong. He may even be committed to the honesty principle. But this ethical statement has no power in and of itself to stop him from lying. It is, after all, still just an idea. In fact, the principle may even compound his problem. Every time the man lies he will feel gulity. The stronger his commitment to the ethic, the more paralyzing the guilt. What this man needs is a different commitment, one that will help him deal with the problem and not simply condemn him. This again points to Jesus, the One Who gave us these principles in the first place and Who promises to give us the power to live them out.

Commitment to community is another step in the right direction. This moves an individual out of the sphere of ideas into the world of relationships; into contact with helping, sharing, forgiving, burden-bearing human beings. Yet even this form of commitment has its limitations. For one thing, it can be selfish. Such a commitment may extend merely to a limited, chosen few—others who are "like us." It is not unknown for groups to be self-centered, exclusive cliques, existing solely for their own ends; reinforcing each other's prejudices and isolating the members from the world at large.

What one really needs is commitment to people in general. This is a commitment which can absorb our whole being; our ideas, our ethics, our love. In fact, it is this sort of commitment which often prepares us for that final commitment to Jesus Christ.

It does this in a strange way. When we discover the liberating fact that we are meant to give ourselves in outflowing love to the people around us, this often generates a strong surge of energy. But this energy does not last forever. After a while we begin to find our giving is not quite so unconditional as it once was. We now get angry on occasion at those we are serving so selflessly. We begin to feel that they are taking advantage of us. And so it goes. Unless we are careful the end result will be bitterness. It is at this point that it dawns on us that in and of ourselves we simply do not have enough resources to give out constantly. We do not have enough patience, enough understanding, enough forgiveness, enough wisdom, enough love. In short, we need help.

It is this very help we find in Jesus. As we give ourselves to Him, He gives Himself to us. In Him we find forgiveness, acceptance, and love, and this in turn enables us to forgive, accept, and love others. We also find new spiritual power. We find we are becoming more patient. We experience moments when we have just the right insight for a particular situation and we can't imagine how we got that idea. We discover, in fact, that as a result of our relationship with Jesus there flows the sort of love which we could never claim as our own. It is not uncommon for a commitment to people (which itself may be based upon a commitment to Christian ideas) to lead us to the point where we realize for the first time that full Christian commitment entails a personal relationship with Jesus.

All this is not to say that if one is committed to Jesus, then commitment in each of the other areas is unnecessary. Nothing could be further from the truth. In this chapter my concern has been with the *initial* commitment, the forms that commitment may take, and the likelihood that they will point us to commitment to Jesus. Commitment, however, opens up a whole world of possibilities which must be explored in depth. This, in fact, is what the Christian life is all about—the ongoing exploration of the areas of our commitment—a subject to which we will return. But, biblically speaking, one does not become a Christian by commitment to Christian truth, to Christian ethics, to the Christian church, nor to other people. One becomes a Christian by commitment to Jesus Christ. Of course, this makes sense when you think about it. It is obviously far better to be committed to the man about Whom the doctrine speaks, Who originated the ethical principles, in Whose name the community gathers; and Who gives us the inner power that enables us truly to love other people. To that encounter we next turn our attention.

▶ Inter Action

Commitments

The Christian life can be thought of as a series of inter-connecting commitments. Although for the sake of analysis I have spoken of these various areas as if they were each separate, in fact they are all interdependent. For example, because of our commitment to Christian ideas we have a certain understanding of the nature of man (he is a fallen being for whom it is vital to be reconciled to the God who loves him). This understanding provides the basis for how we relate to people—which is another of our commitments (we seek to love them as God loves them and are anxious to help them re-discover God). Our commitment to Christian ethics gives additional insights into how to relate to persons (*e.g.*, we seek no one's harm, are honest in our dealing, etc.); as does our commitment to Christian fellowship (*e.g.*, we learn to bear one another's burdens).

Since there is inter-dependence between our various commitments, failure in one area is bound to affect the other areas. For example, this is the reason, I think, that "humanitarian love for people" so often fails when it is a commitment made in isolation from other commitments. We find that with all the will in the world we do not have resources enough by ourselves to go on giving in love indefinitely. We need to be committed to Jesus in order to carry out our commitment to people.

So it is important to examine each of these five areas of commitment. Perhaps our failure to grow is related to deficiencies in one area or another.

I. Spheres of Commitment

A. Think about your commitment to Christian ideas (doctrine); to Christian ethics; to the Christian community; and to people in general.

B. Taking each area one by one, examine your commitment using the following questions. Record your response in your notebook.

1. How did you come to be committed in that sphere? Was this a commitment you came to quickly? Was it the outcome of long deliberation? Was it gradual?

2. Examine the major lines of growth in this area. How has your understanding deepened? How has this affected the way you live?

3. Discuss where you are, right now, in this area. What are you learning at this point?

C. Are there gaps in your commitment? Think about these.

II. Re-commitment: An Exercise in Inner Dialogue

Most of us have carried on imaginary dialogues at some point in our life. Perhaps we are so mad at someone that we find ourselves "telling him off" in our mind, since he is not around to be confronted in person. Or we are preparing for a difficult committee meeting so we sit down and imagine what each person will say to the proposal we must present. We hear ourselves responding to their objections, and then listen to counter-objections—and so rehearse in our minds the whole situation.

Psychologists have found that our ability to engage in inner dialogue gives them a valuable tool in helping individuals come into contact with inner thoughts and feelings. By means of this technique people can be helped to confront aspects of their life where there are problems or uncertainties.

There are many variations to this technique, but in essence all we need to do is to "personify" in our mind who or what it is we want to talk to. We can dialogue with other people, with events in our past, with our career, with a dream image, with a famous person, etc. Here, for example, is the beginning of a dialogue with our body!

(You) "Hello, body. . . ."

(Your body) "Boy, are you abusing me. . . ."

(You) "That's no way to begin a conversation . . .!"

(Body) "Well, I'm sorry, but before we can talk you have to know how I feel. You eat too much."

(You) "I guess so, but. . . ."

(Body) "Guess so! I weigh 210 pounds now and look at me . . .!"

This will strike some people as very strange behavior, but I suggest you try this technique for yourself. Don't worry about the fact that you are "making up" the dialogue. Of course you are—and this is the reason that this technique yields such insights into your real feelings and thoughts. As Ira Progoff has noted: "Rereading our dialogue scripts, it is not uncommon to find that information that is significantly new to us has been stated in them or to recognize that attitudes of long-standing have been transformed in them. . . ."[3] When we engage in such dialogue we are coming in touch with inner processes deeper than consciousness.

I suggest you try a dialogue with that area of your commitment which is the weakest. Do this by finding a quiet place where you will not be disturbed. Take out a piece of paper and write on the top of it the "personification" with which you want to dialogue (*e.g.*, "Commitment to People"). Then sit back. Close your eyes. Let yourself become quiet. After a moment or two gradually open yourself to this partner in dialogue. Let your mind come into contact with this area of life. Don't try to direct your thoughts, just "feel" what is there. Greet your partner.

Let him speak. Write down the conversation.

It will be important to keep your attention focused inward. Do not pay any more than mechanical attention to the writing.

When you draw the "conversation" to a close, sit back and try to record how you felt as you dialogued. Put down those random impressions, insights, feelings.

At some later time, go back to the script which you have produced. Read it over again. As you do so, once again put down the impressions and feelings that come to you. Finally, focus on what you have learned out of all this, particularly concerning the problem you have in this area and the possibility for future growth.

When you are all done, make up a new section in your Growth Notebook, entitled, "Inner Dialogue" and file your work there.

7 Encounter

In the January 26, 1975 edition of *The New York Times Magazine*, Father Andrew Greely and Dr. William McCready published a fascinating article entitled "Are We a Nation of Mystics?"[1] In it, they report on the results of a representative survey conducted by the National Opinion Research Center of the University of Chicago. The aim of the survey was to probe the question of ultimate values. However, because of their curiosity (and, I suppose, the fact that they are both practicing Catholics) Greely and McCready managed to squeeze in a handful of questions concerning mystical experiences. What they hoped to find out was how many people in American society have had mystical experiences, what types of people were likely to have them, and what impact such experiences had on their lives. Specifically they asked the respondents: "Have you ever had the feeling of being very close to a powerful spiritual force that seemed to lift you out of yourself?"—a question which touched upon the core of such experiences as described in mystical literature.

To their amazement 40% replied that yes, indeed, they had had such experiences. Greely and McCready's conclusion: "We have a substantial segment of the American population who have had intense spiritual experiences."

Most people, when they hear about "mystical experiences," immediately think of the Middle Ages and individuals like Saint Bernard of Clairvaux and Meister Eckhart. So it comes as a real surprise when we hear that according to this survey four out of every ten American adults living today have had a mystical experience. Why didn't we know this before? Certainly some of our friends must have had such an experience. The answer is that virtually none of the respondents had mentioned their experience to anyone, not even to spouse, friend, or clergyman. Given the temper of our age, as one respondent put it: "It just didn't seem to be the kind of thing people talk about." Yet most of the respondents considered the experience one of the most important things that had ever happened in their lives.

Such mystical experiences are important for our consideration because they often lead to conversion, *i.e.,* to the decision on our part to start following Jesus. This should not be surprising. Given the fact that in such experiences we become aware of the reality and power of the living God, the decision to start following His ways would seem the most natural response.

However, this is not the inevitable response. Not all those who have mystical experiences become followers of Christ. It is possible to go through a mystical experience, be profoundly moved by it, but then merely set it aside never allowing the implications of this encounter to be felt in our on-going life. An experience alone is not enough no matter how tinged with the supernatural it might be. We must respond to it. We must open ourselves to the meaning of the experience in such a way that it is integrated into our life. We must say "Yes" to this vision of God: "Yes, I will recognize the reality of God (faith) and I will alter my life to fit in with the implications of this reality (repentance)." It is the saying "Yes" that results in conversion.

Conversion, or encounter with Christ, is found on the Pilgrimage chart between the end of the Commitment phase and the beginning of the Integration phase. It merits a chapter on its own because it is such a decisive element in the whole of pilgrimage. This is the experience toward which all of the movement in the Quest and Commitment phases points and from which subsequent growth as a Christian follows. Without this encounter with Christ the direction of our life and growth will be quite different. In fact, according to Scripture, without this encounter our experience of "wholeness" will be incomplete, the whole spiritual side of our nature having been denied. Hence, the need to examine in such detail this one particular point in our overall pilgrimage. In fact, in many ways, our real pilgrimage only begins with commitment to Christ. At this point the god-ward motion in our life is confirmed and our goal given specific definition. Henceforth it will be a matter of growing ever more in conformity with the image of Christ to whom we have pledged our lives.

Not everyone has mystical experiences. This was also clear from the survey. Six out of ten Americans have known no such overpowering inner awareness as characterizes these experiences. However, this does not mean that therefore it is impossible for non-mystics to make a Christian commitment. While conversion arising out of a mystical encounter (*à la* Saint Paul on the Damascus Road) is the most dramatic form of such an experience, it is not the only possible means of coming to God. In fact, conversion happens in a variety of ways.

A friend of mine, while a high school student, committed her life to Christ. For quite some time she had considered taking this step. She had carefully thought through the pros and cons and finally concluded that she did indeed want to follow Jesus. So, one Sunday evening, at the conclusion of the worship service, she went to the front of the church in response to the routinely given invitation to come forward if one wanted to make a commitment to Jesus. Then and there she committed her life to Christ. She had no particular emotional experience at the time or later on. She had never had a mystical experience. She went forward solely as the result of having thought through the issues. Her experience was what I call "cognitive conversion," *i.e.*, conversion arising primarily as a result of an intellectual decision.

The experience of Dan Young was quite different.

> One morning, being in deep distress, fearing every moment I should drop into hell, I was constrained to cry in earnest for mercy, and the Lord came to my relief, and delivered my soul from the burden and guilt of sin. My whole frame was in a tremor from head to foot, and my soul enjoyed sweet peace. The pleasure I then felt was indescribable. The happiness lasted about three days, during which time I never spoke to any person about my feelings.[2]

Here, emotion, not thought, dominated. I know nothing more about Dan Young than what I read in this short quote taken from William James, but I assume he went on to be a loyal follower of Jesus Christ. The existence of what appears to be a religious autobiography would seem to indicate, that in fact he contributed significantly to the on-going work of the Kingdom. In any case, his experience of an emotional conversion is not unique. Countless people have begun their Christian life in an identical way—in tears, with a great emotional swing from despair to joy.

The conversion of Charles Finney, the great American evangelist, combined intellectual, emotional, and mystical elements.

> When I came to Adams to study law, I was almost as ignorant of religion as a heathen. I had been brought up mostly in the woods. I had very little regard for the Sabbath, and had no definite knowledge of religious truth. . . . At Adams, for the first time, I sat steadily for a length of time under an educated ministry. . . . I was not able to gain very much instruction from his (Mr. Gale's) preaching. . . . I was more perplexed than edified by his preaching.
>
> In studying elementary law, I found the old authors frequently quoting the Scriptures. . . . This excited my curiosity so much that I went and purchased a Bible. . . . I read and meditated on it much more than I had ever done before in my life. . . . But as I read my Bible and attended prayer meeting, heard Mr. Gale preach and conversed with him, I became very restless. . . . It seemed to me that there must be something in religion that was of infinite importance; and it was soon settled with me, that if the soul was immortal, I needed a great change in my inward state to be prepared for the happiness of heaven. But still my mind was not made up as to the truth or falsehood of the Gospel and the Christian religion. The question,

however, was of too much importance to allow me to rest in any uncertainty on the subject. . . .

This being settled, I was brought face to face with the question whether I would accept Christ as presented in the Gospel or pursue a worldly course of life. At this period, my mind, as I have since known, was so much impressed by the Holy Spirit, that I could not long leave this question unsettled; nor could I long hesitate between two courses of life presented to me. . . .

On a Sabbath evening in the autumn of 1821, I made up my mind that I would settle the question of my soul's salvation at once, that if it were possible I would make my peace with God. . . . But I was very proud without knowing it. . . . After I addressed myself in earnest to the subject of my own salvation, I kept my Bible as much as I could out of sight. . . . During Monday and Tuesday, my conviction increased; but it seemed as if my heart grew harder. I could not shed a tear, I could not pray. . . . Tuesday night, I had become very nervous; and in the night a strange feeling came over me as if I were about to die. I knew that if I did I should sink down into hell. . . .

Just at this point, the whole question of Gospel salvation opened up to me in a manner most marvellous to me at the time. I think then I saw as clearly as I ever have in my life, the reality and fullness of the atonement of Christ. . . .

Without being distinctly aware of it, I had stopped in the street right where the inward voice seemed to arrest me. How long I remained in this position I cannot say. But after this distinct revelation had stood for some time before my mind, the question seemed to be put, "Will you accept it now, today?" I replied, "Yes, I will accept it today or die in the attempt. . . ."

I turned and bent my course toward the woods, feeling that I must be alone, and away from human eyes and ears, so that I could pour out my prayer to God. . . .

Finally I found myself verging fast to despair. . . .

Just at this moment I again thought I heard someone approach me and I opened my eyes to see whether it were so. . . . The sin appeared awful, infinite. It broke me down before the Lord.

I had intellectually believed the Bible before; but never had the truth been in my mind that faith was a voluntary trust instead of an intellectual state. . . .

I prayed till my mind became so full that, before I was aware of it, I was on my feet tripping up the ascent toward the road. . . . I soon reached the road that led to the village and began to reflect upon what had passed; and I found that my mind had become most wonderfully quiet and peaceful.

Later on that day Finney reported that:

I received a mighty baptism of the Holy Ghost. Without any expectation of it, without ever having thought in my mind that there was such a thing for me. Without any recollection that I had ever heard the thing mentioned by any person in the world, [sic] seemed to go through me, body and soul.

No words can express the wonderful love that was shed abroad in my heart.[3]

A third type of conversion experience is characterized not so much by a dominant psychological process (*e.g.*, thought or emotion) but by the fact that it takes place over a long period of time rather than at one given moment as in the above examples. Of course, it can be argued (correctly) that probably these so-called "sudden" experiences were preceeded by a period of preparation—conscious or unconscious—which then culminated in a decisive act of commitment. Nevertheless, it is also true that many people are not aware of ever having one experience to which they can point and say: "Then and there I decided to follow Jesus." Rather, when they look back on their lives they realize that they have been in the process of turning to Christ for quite some time and in fact do now trust Him. What they can look back on is not a definite conversion experience but rather the moment of insight when they realized that they were indeed following Christ. Some people do not even have this experience of insight because they cannot ever recall a time when they did not believe in Jesus and seek to follow Him. As Dr. R. W. Dale put it in a series of papers he wrote on the relation of children to the Church:

There are not a few who can testify that "from their childhood," they knew not "the Scriptures" but God Himself; they came to know Him they cannot know how; . . . they knew Him before they could understand any name by which in our imperfect human speech we have endeavored to affirm His goodness, His power, or His glory.[4]

Sudden or gradual; mystical, intellectual, or emotional—the type of experience varies from person to person. What is common, however, is the awareness of a commitment to Christ that unlocks the final phase of Christian pilgrimage: the on-going integration of Christian realities into our daily life.

But how, specifically, do we commit ourselves to Jesus? What are the dynamics of this encounter? Do we merely say, "O.K., Jesus, I believe in you," and that's that? Or do we have to wait until some sort of overwhelming experience of God overtakes us? Or is it just matter of trying to live a Christian life as best we can?

In fact, there are two distinct responses which come together to characterize commitment to Christ: repentance and faith. Right from the beginning of His ministry Jesus made it plain that He was calling men and women to such a two-fold response. Here is how Mark summarizes Jesus' preaching at the start of His ministry.

Now after John was arrested, Jesus came into Galilee, preaching the Gospel of God, and saying, "the time is fulfilled, and the Kingdom of God is at hand; *repent, and believe in the Gospel.*" Mark 1:14-15

To repent means literally to "change one's mind." In order to come to Christ we have to change our minds about the direction in which our life is going. We have to decide that we will stop living our life in the manner we have up to that point, *i.e.,* we stop following our own whims and inclinations; and instead, start following Christ's way. Whereas we once lived apart from God and the demands of His Kingdom, now it is our desire to become a part of that Kingdom.

There are at least four aspects to repentance. It involves a *recognition* of the inadequacy of our former perspective; a *regret* over all the wrong done; a *request* for pardon and forgiveness; and a *resolve* to live a new life. This is repentance as understood in theological terms. The actual experience of repentance varies from person to person. Different people come to realize the inadequacy of their basic life orientation in different ways. For some of us, this arises out of dissatisfaction. Perhaps a long sought after goal is reached, yet this accomplishment fails to bring the satisfaction we had anticipated, so we wonder if there is more to life than striving after a goal. Or perhaps we have just had an encounter with a book or a person. As a result, we have seen ourselves as we really are, and are dismayed. We do not like what we see and we wonder if we really can become what we know we should be. Perhaps it is a sense of guilt that prompts our longing to change; or it may be anxiety about death or fear of the unknown future. No matter what the specific cause, our dissatisfaction drives us to seek a way of forgiveness, a path of renewal, a means of grace whereby we can become what we sense we ought to be.

For others of us, it is a sense of longing that opens the door to repentance. We know there is meant to be more in life. Now and then we catch glimpses of the More and these serve to heighten our desire to be part of whatever this is. As C. S. Lewis expressed it: "Our lifelong nostalgia, our longing to be re-united with something in the universe from which we now feel cut off, to be on the inside of some door which we have always seen from the·outside; is no mere neurotic fancy, but the truest index of our real situation."[5] We long to participate in the richness of life which has thus far eluded us. And so we willingly give up our past life-style when we discover that which is truer and more in touch with reality.

Despite its significance, repentance is not a word that we use very much. For many people, it has become synonymous with weeping sinners kneeling by an altar rail at the end of a sawdust trail. (Repentance *may* involve emotion, especially when we suddenly "see" how destructive our past has been and are overwhelmed by this vision of all the wrong we have done. This sorrow, however, is not repentance. It is a serious mistake to equate repentance with an emotion that sometimes accompanies it.) However, despite the semantic problems, individuals do continue to *experience* repentance. From a hundred different vantage points, they come to see the inadequacy of a life lived apart from God. They regret all the hurt done to others and to themselves as a result of living a self-centered existence, and they seek God's forgiveness as they resolve to lead a new life. This is the experience of repentance which is part of any life-changing encounter with Jesus.

Repentance, however, is not *equivalent* to commitment. It is only an element. In and of itself, it is incomplete, because repentance that is not linked with faith is nothing more than a "good resolution." It is in the appropriation of the power of the Gospel that a changed life becomes possible. Repentance indicates our willingness to change our life-style and follow Christ. The Gospel gives us His power actually to do so.

What is this "Gospel" or "Good News" which we are called upon to believe? In Mark 1:15, the "Good News" is that the Kingdom of God has finally come. However, after Christ's death and resurrection, it became evident that the Gospel included not only the announcement of the Kingdom but the news that Christ has provided the means whereby each and every person can be a part of this Kingdom. In 1 Cor. 15, Saint Paul summarizes this Gospel in this way:

> Now I would remind you, brethren, in what terms I preached to you the gospel, which you received, in which you stand, by which you are saved, if you hold it fast—unless you believed in vain. For I delivered to you as of first importance what I also received, that Christ died for our sins in accordance with the scriptures, that he was buried, that he was raised on the third day in accordance with the scriptures, and that he appeared to Cephas, then to the twelve. Then he appeared to more than five hundred brethren at one time, most of whom are still alive, though some have fallen asleep. (1 Cor. 15:1-6)

In other words, the Gospel consists of certain historical facts about Jesus (*e.g.,* "he was raised") and at least one interpretation of these facts (*i.e.,* "he died *for our sins*"). In believing these facts we are giving assent to Jesus' claim to be God incarnate; for if He did indeed rise from the dead, He is most certainly who He claimed to be. In believing that His death was *for our sins,* we are trusting in Him to forgive us and to give us the power to live a new life.

In the act of repentance we are brought face to face with our real self—the self living apart from God, and with the realization that we can do nothing to alter our sin-prone nature. Now by faith we believe this nature can be healed because, Jesus, the Son of God, died for our sins. But what about the act of believing itself? It involves intellectual acceptance to be sure. No one will deliberately give himself to a lie. But "belief" or "faith" in the New Testament goes beyond mere assent to a set of propositions. It also involves action. A man who is truly sorry about his past life and trusts in Jesus to forgive him and to give him power to lead a new life, will *live differently* than he did prior to his act of commitment. Otherwise, he is fooling himself that he has truly repented and really believed in Christ.

At its very core, in this act of repentance and faith, we are brought face to face with the living Christ. We are not committing ourselves to a creed, to an institution, to a style of piety. We are committing ourselves to a Person—to the Person, Jesus, who died but rose again and yet lives.

> Mere intellectual assent to facts does not make a person a Christian any more than mere intellectual assent to facts makes a person married. Many people's dissatisfaction with Christianity is because they are like a person who says: "I believe in marriage, I'm sold on marriage, I've read a dozen books on marriage, and in the last three months I've been to fifteen weddings, but for some strange reason marriage doesn't mean anything to me." The reason is very simple: he isn't married. Marriage is not a philosophy . . . nor is Christianity . . . rather it is a dynamic relationship with a living person, the Lord Jesus Christ. Just as getting married means giving up our independence, so does receiving Christ. The essence of sin is living independently of God—going my way rather than His way. The essence of repentance is the repudiation of the self-centered principle making Christ and His will the centre of my life. When we marry we think of another person in all our decisions. When we receive Christ, we enter into a consultative relationship with Him about every area of our lives.[6]

▶ Inter Action

Meeting Jesus

The aim of this exercise is to recall that time in your life when you committed yourself to Jesus. This may have taken the form of a "sudden experience;" it may have been more a matter of "finally" realizing that you were committed to Jesus; or it may be that you cannot recall ever not following Jesus. Whatever the specific shape of your experience, try to recall that period in your life by means of the following questions.

I. Preparation
What factors in your life led you to the point that you wanted to follow Jesus? Dissatisfaction? Longing? Fear? Try to note as specifically as possible all the various inputs that combined to create this "divine dissatisfaction" in your life.

II. Causes
What was the precipitating cause that led you to the actual experience of commitment? A mystical experience? An intellectual decision? An emotional experience?

If this was a mystical experience, try to express what happened as best you can. Then, consider sharing your experience with others. In fact, your own openness could well free others to "confess" to a similar encounter and perhaps motivate them to think through the implication of this experience for their lives.

III. The Experience Itself
Now describe the experience of conversion—however it occurred. Note particularly the nature of your faith-response.

By way of an example, here is how two Christian writers describe their conversion experience. First there is Professor C. S. Lewis, who was able to come to Christianity only after his *mind* was convinced Christianity was true.

> Then I read Chesterton's *Everlasting Man* and for the first time saw the whole Christian outline of history set out in a form that seemed to me to make sense. Somehow I contrived not to be too badly shaken. You will remember that I already thought Chesterton the most sensible man alive "apart from his Christianity." Now, I veritably believe, I thought—I didn't of course *say;* words would have revealed the nonsense—that Christianity

itself was very sensible "apart from its Christianity." But I hardly remember, for I had not long finished *The Everlasting Man* when something
far more alarming happened to me. Early in 1926 the hardest boiled of all
the atheists I ever knew sat in my room on the other side of the fire and
remarked that the evidence for the historicity of the Gospels was really
surprisingly good. "Rum thing," he went on. "All that stuff of Frazer's about
the Dying God. Rum thing. It almost looks as if it had really happened
once." To understand the shattering impact of it, you would need to know
the man (who has certainly never since shown any interest in Christianity).
If he, the cynic of cynics, the toughest of toughs, were not—as I would still
have put it—"safe," where could I turn? Was there then no escape?

The odd thing was that before God closed in on me, I was in fact offered
what now appears a moment of wholly free choice. In a sense. I was going
up Headington Hill on the top of a bus. Without words and (I think) almost
without images, a fact was somehow presented to me. I became aware that
I was holding something at bay, or shutting something out. Or, if you like,
that I was wearing some stiff clothing, like corsets, or even a suit of
armour, as if I were a lobster. I felt myself being, there and then, given a
free choice. I could open the door or keep it shut; I could unbuckle the
armour or keep it on. Neither choice was presented as a duty; no threat or
promise was attached to either, though I knew that to open the door or to
take off the corslet meant the incalculable. The choice appeared to be
momentous but it was also strangely unemotional. I was moved by no
desires or fears. In a sense I was not moved by anything. I chose to open,
to unbuckle, to loosen the rein. I say, "I chose," yet it did not really seem
possible to do the opposite. On the other hand, I was aware of no motives.
You could argue that I was not a free agent, but I am more inclined to think
that this came nearer to being a perfectly free act than most I have ever
done. Necessity may not be the opposite of freedom, and perhaps a man is
most free when, instead of producing motives, he could only say, "I am
what I do." Then came the repercussion on the imaginative level. I felt as if
I were a man of snow at long last beginning to melt. The melting was
starting in my back—drip-drip and presently trickle-trickle. I rather disliked
the feeling.[7]

Lewis describes the completion of this process:

You must picture me alone in that room at Magdalen, night after night,
feeling, whenever my mind lifted for a second from my work, the steady,
unrelenting approach of Him whom I so earnestly desired not to meet. That
which I greatly feared had at last come upon me. In the Trinity Term of
1929 I gave in, and admitted that God was God, and knelt and prayed:
perhaps, that night, the most dejected and reluctant convert in all England.
I did not then see what is now the most shining and obvious thing; the
Divine humility which will accept a convert even on such terms. The
Prodigal Son at least walked home on his own feet. But who can duly adore
that Love which will open the high gates to a prodigal who is brought in
kicking, struggling, resentful, and darting his eyes in every direction for a
chance of escape? The words *compelle intrare*, compel them to come in,

have been so abused by wicked men that we shudder at them; but properly understood, they plumb the depth of the Divine mercy. The hardness of God is kinder than the softness of men, and His compulsion is our liberation.[8]

John Stott writes of his experience in the third person, quoting extracts from his childhood diary:

A boy in his later teens knelt at his bedside one Sunday night in the dormitory of his public school. It was about 10 p.m. on 13 February 1928. In a simple, matter-of-fact but definite way he told Christ that he had made rather a mess of his life so far; he confessed his sins; he thanked Christ for dying for him; and he asked Him to come into his life. The following day he wrote in his diary: "Yesterday really *was* an eventful day! . . . Up till now Christ has been on the circumference and I have but asked Him to guide me instead of giving Him complete control. Behold! He stands at the door and knocks. I have heard Him and now is He come into my house. He has cleansed it and now rules therein. . . ." And the day after: "I really have felt an immense and new joy throughout today. It is the joy of being at peace with the world and of being in touch with God. How well do I know now that He rules me and that I never really knew Him before. . . ."[9]

IV. Expressing the Experience

Now draw together the strands of your experience into a whole statement of some sort. For example, you might want to write out the story of your experience. You could do this in novel form with the emphasis on dialogue, as a poem, as an allegory, or as a straight essay. Or you might try doing a drawing—with water colors or felt-tipped pen—which will express what happened to you. Whatever form you choose, let your creative energies flow in expressing the significance to you of this "Grand Encounter."

After your work is complete, sit back, and record what happened to you during the creative process itself. What new insights did you gain? What feelings did you experience? Were there any intimations of what that past experience could mean in your present life?

Repentance/Faith Images

By way of preparation for this chapter:

1. Close your eyes for a moment, and think about repentance. What images come to your mind? By means of a word or phrase, make a note of these images on a scrap of paper. (In a few minutes you will get the chance to develop the images more thoroughly. For now, just write down enough so as not to forget.) Let the pictures grow and develop in your mind. What is the essence of repentance? Imagine someone repenting. Recall your own experience of repentance. Don't worry if the images are funny, negative, or incomplete. Just try to grab on to the various ideas which are aroused in your mind when you hear the word "repent."

2. Now expand these images and ideas. You can do this using words, pictures, doodles, whatever. The aim of this exercise is to help you clarify in your own mind how you think about repentance. Once you have completed this image-expansion, try to sum up how you understand repentance (i.e., write out a definition) and, even more importantly, how you feel about the word (i.e., are your images negative? positive?).

3. Now go through exactly the same process with the concept of "faith." Get in touch with your inner images and ideas about faith. Expand these, and then write out some sort of definition of faith.

8 Integration

It was one of our more dramatic small group meetings. Jane (I'll call her) was a fairly new member of the group. Although she had been a Christian for some time, her experience in this area as in most other areas of her life, had been stormy. Divorced, living in a small apartment with a job that would soon end, she was lonely, depressed, and suicidal. The group tried, in its small way, to care for Jane.

On the evening in question, Jane had arrived in great spirits. Something had happened and she wanted to tell us about it. We set aside the planned agenda and Jane launched into her story. It seemed that she had experienced one of those rare but decisive encounters with God out of which came new and crucial insight into who she was and what was going on in her life. All alone one evening, she became aware of God's presence and with it a sense that many of her problems could be traced to her failure to take God seriously in one particular area: her sexual life. She knew in a deep and decisive way that she must give up her promiscuity in order to get back on the road to health and wholeness. It was a revelation that had made sense to her.

Listening to Jane that evening, we all got the feeling that she was a newly freed woman. She was open, articulate, and happy. She did not feel the need to hide anything. She had faced herself and seen what was really there. And she had accepted this insight from God not as a condemning judgment but as a guidance from a loving Father. She had asked and was assured of His forgiveness. And she had put this sinful pattern of living behind her. The result of all this was that now she had hope.

It struck me then (and we discussed it in the group that evening) that here was a classic (albeit dramatic) example of what repentance and faith is all about. It began with *insight* into the way things really were. Jane had become *aware* of a hitherto unevaluated but destructive pattern of living. Insight had then been followed by a decision to *change*. She decided to stop sleeping around. This change was *made possible* because Jane sensed God's love for her (not His condemnation); because she *believed* that He would forgive her if she would but ask; and because the Holy Spirit would assist her in carrying out her intentions.

I was also struck by the result of this act of repentance and faith. By aligning herself with the way she ought to be living, she found new freedom and hope. Repentance and faith had led toward wholeness.

I hope that it is clear by now that repentance and faith are key at every point in the Christian pilgrimage. During the Quest phase, each step of movement becomes possible only after the question of need and the question of belief are resolved. An individual must *want to change* his point of view, having seen inadequacy in his former perspective (repentance), and he has got to *believe* that the new viewpoint is more in touch with reality. Likewise, commitment to Christ takes place when a person realizes that he has not been following Jesus but now wants to do so (repentance) and that he can in fact be forgiven for his past and begin following Jesus as a result of his trust (faith) in Jesus who died and rose again. In the Christian life also, we move forward via repentance and faith. It is not surprising that Martin Luther focused on repentance in the first of the 95 theses that he tacked to the door of the church in Wittenberg on that All Saints Eve in 1517: "Our Lord and Master Jesus Christ, when He said, Repent, willed that the whole life of believers should be repentance." Nor that he then went on to open up a whole new understanding of the nature of faith in the life of the Christian.

Since it is not always recognized that repentance and faith are as essential to Christian growth as they are to Christian conversion,[1] it is important to consider in detail how these two responses relate to the on-going life of the Christian.

As I indicated earlier, the root meaning of repentance is "to change one's mind." But before we can "change our minds" (about the way we are living or thinking), we first have to be made aware that a change is in order. In other words, repentance begins with *insight*. It does not matter whether the insight is negative ("something is wrong") or positive ("there is a better way"). The important thing is that we have come to realize that the *status quo* may not be best. Insight has opened up the option of change.

Insight is like a spotlight. It shines into various corners of our life and reveals what is really there. For example, insight reveals to us the real meaning and implications of our actions. King David, in his lust for Bathsheba, arranged for her husband Uriah to be killed in battle. The implications of what he had done did not strike David until God sent Nathan the prophet to tell him the story of the poor man's one ewe lamb. By means of a prophet, insight came to David as to the significance of his actions, and so he repented.

Insight also illuminates our thoughts. All of us have wrong-headed notions about a great many things. This is just a fact of being human and hence very fallible, and we would all acknowledge that the clearer our understanding the better we are able to order our lives in this world.

Insight illuminates our attitudes as well. Attitudes are very difficult to get at, since they are comprised of feelings as well as thoughts. Often we are at a loss to explain why we relate to certain people as we do. We just do. Hence the importance of insight to elucidate this crucial area of our life. In any case, be it our actions, thoughts, or attitudes, we can only change when we come to *see* in a new way what is going on in that area of our life.

But insight is not easily attained. All of us live in a state of partial blindness. We are unaware of what is really going on in whole areas of our life. It is not that we choose blindness (though this does sometimes happen). It is simply that we cannot see. Our culture, our experiences, our family and our education all conspire together to create our views of the world. The gaps are not there by planning but simply by dint of our being human and hence limited.

One major reason for these gaps in our perspective is that we have never seen anyone think or behave differently in these particular areas. So naturally we assume that the familiar pattern is the only pattern. We have no foil against which to judge our thoughts or behavior. To my mind, this lack of alternative models accounts in part for the appalling blindness in South Africa when it comes to relationships between the races. Isolated on the southern tip of Africa, with hostile black nations to the north and Europe thousands of miles away, the average South African, be he black or white, has little opportunity to encounter positive relationships between people of differing races. Hence white and black continue to relate as they have related for 200 years—as superior to inferior. They do not know any other pattern and fear coupled with misunderstanding prevents most from seeking a new way. On more than one occasion my wife and I have seen gracious, generous white South African Christians, while in the process of being immensely kind to us, turn around and without thought treat a black servant as if he were dirt—all the time *totally unaware of what they were doing.*

But our blindness is not due solely to the absence of other alternatives. It can also be a case of our own inner defenses coming into play. The human psyche is a marvellous thing. Built into it are incredible mechanisms which serve to preserve it from dissolution. Yet these very necessary defense mechanisms can themselves become the problem, by shutting us off from insights vital to our growth. For example, a person comes to us with a grievance. Perhaps we have been treating a mutual friend unfairly. But if we sense any judgment on the part of the person bearing this news, our instinctive reaction is to defend ourselves, and thereby deny what might be a perfectly valid insight.

So far, our discussion of repentance has focused on the necessity and nature of insight. It has undoubtedly occurred to you that while we have acknowledged that there are blockages to insight, we have yet to deal with the difficult problem of obtaining insight. This is, in fact, the subject of Chapters 11 and 12. But our present topic is repentance, and that requires that we face the equally difficult problem of dealing with those insights we already have.

There are two basic responses to insight. We can say "Yes" or we can say "No." If we say "Yes" and thus acknowledge the correctness of the insight, we have opened up to ourselves the possibility of change. If we say "No," we choose instead to remain where we are, and risk the deadliness of stagnation.

While "Yes" is a straight-forward response, there are various ways of saying "No." We can, for example, simply refuse to accept the accuracy of the insight. "No, that is wrong, that is not true, that is not the way it is with me." Or we can rationalize what we hear and explain away what may be perfectly true. "Well, you may have a point there, but what you fail to understand is. . . ." It is also possible to see and accept the truth of an insight, but then simply fail to do anything about it. This is particularly dangerous because it sets up a dichotomy between our thoughts and our actions. This happens at times when we mistake our emotional responses for real change. We see something with devastating clarity, and feel awful about it for a time, but in fact we do nothing to change our way of living, wrongly concluding that "feeling bad" is what repentance is all about. Sometimes even our theology can get in the way of on-going repentance: "I repented when I became a Christian, so why do I need to repent again?" Whatever the form of our "No," we need to ask whether it prevents us from growing ever more in conformity with what Jesus intends us to be.

This is not to say that all new insights are correct. We must use our God-given judgment in assessing what is or is not true. Otherwise we abdicate *our* responsibility for following Christ and put ourselves at the mercy of others. So, in fact, we will have to say "No" to some insights, not out of pride which does not allow us to admit any inadequacy, but simply because, in our best judgment, the insight is wrong or not applicable to us.

It is also true that sometimes we are *not ready* for a particular insight. What we are confronted with may be true, but for one reason or another, we are not able to accept it. Or, if we do, we are not able to make it part of our life. For example, when I first went to South Africa, I knew from a variety of sources that the way blacks were treated there was wrong. While I accepted this on a theoretical level, it did not have the force of a central, driving insight. I believed *apartheid* was wrong, but this idea did not really affect me very much. Eventually, however, we got to know black South Africans, and as they grew to know and trust us, they gradually shared with us the daily, unrelenting agony that *apartheid* imposed on their lives. I began to see that *apartheid* was not simply another political viewpoint which could be accepted or rejected. It was a brutal form of oppression that ground the very humanity out of millions of people. At this point, the insight that *apartheid* was wrong became more than theoretical. It began to affect the way I lived.

As I look back over my life it is evident that there are a whole host of insights which I rejected at first, only to affirm them later after various experiences made it possible to see their validity. It seems to be so that there are times when we have to reject what is true simply because we have not yet reached the point in our life experience where we can see that truth much less accept it. Yet, if our attitude is one of on-going openness, the day will come when we are able to affirm that particular truth.

If it is repentance that opens the possibility of change, then it is faith that actually brings about new growth. There are at least three ways that faith relates to growth. First of all, faith enables us to face ourselves as we really are. By faith we are assured of two vital facts: that God really does love us and that He will actually forgive us. Knowing this, we have the courage to face what is ugly in ourselves. We can look, without hesitation, at those areas of our life that are in need of redemption. Without this assurance of love and forgiveness, our natural tendency is either to shy away from the sort of input that will point out our weaknesses, or to deny that any problem exists.

I think we sometimes forget what an immense plus this trust in God's love and forgiveness brings into our life. God has actually promised that if we but ask, He will forgive us. It is simply impossible for many people to face their real selves because if they admitted their feelings and faults, they could not live with the guilt such an admission would bring. They have no way to cope with that which is destructive within themselves. So they either deny having done anything wrong, or they try to live with a philosophy that says there really is no such thing as right and wrong. Neither strategy works. To foster the sort of blindness that prevents our coming in touch with personal failings simultaneously induces a lack of sensitivity into our life. We grow out of touch with the people around us and the environment in which we live. The result, life with a dull, grey cast, is a high price to pay in order to avoid our weaknesses.

Likewise, the attempt to live as if right and wrong were meaningless categories is also doomed to failure. C. S. Lewis pointed out that there is built deep within the personality of every man, regardless of era or culture, an inner knowledge that some things are right and others wrong.[2] It is fooling ourselves to pretend that this is not so, and any attempt to live this way will eventually catch up with us psychologically. But the Christian knows that forgiveness *is* offered by God. Therefore, he has the freedom, the almost unthinkable freedom, to face the worst in himself, because God has promised real forgiveness.

God has also pledged His unchanging love for us. The Christian, therefore, not only has the assurance that he will be forgiven, he also knows that his actions, no matter how despicable, will not separate him from the love of God. This is not, incidentally, an encouragement to live irresponsibly. We still have to bear the consequences of our actions, both in terms of how they have affected us and what they do to others. As I once heard a college chaplain point out, if an unmarried student gets pregnant, even though she and her partner may seek and find God's forgiveness, this in no way alters the fact of the pregnancy. Yet even in this situation, the freeing sense of this forgiving love can make it possible for the two individuals to cope with the problem in a more effective way than if they were laden with guilt.

There is a second way in which faith relates to personal change. Our faith defines for us the direction in which we ought to change. It is by faith that we accept that the pattern for living set out in Scripture is indeed God's pattern. In the Bible, we have a very concrete idea of the way in which we ought to be living; and hence can seek constantly to adjust our lives in that direction. Without such guidance the nature of our change would be haphazard. We might become aware, for example, that our relationship with our children is in bad shape. We want to change. But how? Without the sort of Scriptural insights into the nature of human relationships in general and into parent and child relationships specifically, the change we initiate might even worsen the situation!

Again, I think we sometimes do not realize how valuable a resource we have as Christians in the Scriptures. The insights in the Bible provide us with the direction we need in order to make sense out of this life. This is quite staggering. We are not left to flounder this way and that, trying desperately to discover what brings wholeness to life. The pattern is there. This is not to say that we always act consistently in accord with Scriptural teachings, or even that we have invested enough energy to learn all there is in the Bible. Nevertheless, the general life directions are there, and by faith we believe them to be from God and hence we can know in what direction change ought to take place.

There is yet a third way in which faith enables change. By faith we open ourselves to those gifts from God that bring about change: the gift of fellowship, the gift of guidance, and the gift of the Holy Spirit.

Very often it is the presence of a fellowshipping community that makes change possible. On our own we are so powerless. We can will all sorts of things, but we never seem to have the power actually to do that which we say we desire. Yet, when we participate in a community of caring, sharing, burden-bearing people we find strength beyond ourselves. At times this comes simply because we have others to whom we can turn in honesty and weakness, knowing that we will not be rejected, but will find a sharing of our problems. At other times, it is the shared ministry of the group that makes all the difference. God gives different people different gifts with the intention that these gifts be used to promote the wholeness of the body. And so we find that the gifts of certain individuals match our particular needs and hence we are enabled to grow.

We have also been promised guidance by God. He *will* lead us, the Bible declares. He has already done this by setting down in Scripture the general patterns for living. But there will come those points when we need a specific word from God. It is then that the "still, small voice" speaking within us makes all the difference. Theodor Bovet, a Swiss psychiatrist, tells us how one goes about the process of listening for God's guiding voice: "It is necessary to have sufficient time at our disposal in order to listen to God out of the deep silence." He then points out that when we start to become silent before God, the first thoughts that emerge will probably relate to daily concerns. We must pay attention to them, he says. However, after a while "thoughts gradually emerge that are strange to us, but nevertheless are convincing because of their inner correctness and their particular luminescence . . . Such is God's guidance. It is not possible adequately to describe this experience, but if one has experienced it a few times then one is aware of the difference."[3] Such inner leading, which we seek and accept by faith, is intimately related to personal change.

Finally, there is the gift of the Holy Spirit Himself. It is He who brings the power that enables us to change. Countless people down through the ages have testified to transformations that have taken place in their lives, brought about by a power they knew was not their own. This is the testimony of scores of alcoholics and drug-dependent individuals who found the power to give up their addiction instantly and forever. This is also the testimony of those who find a new ability to love, or to forgive, or to cope, or to hope, or to trust. Without great effort on their part, simply as a result of an act of faith, they find a new thing in their lives. All this is the work of the Holy Spirit.

This whole subject is fraught with mystery, however. Just as it is clear that the Holy Spirit gives such power, it is also clear that He cannot be manipulated or even anticipated. Two alcoholics pray the same prayer with the same faith, and one is released immediately from his addiction while the other may have to struggle for years to overcome his compulsion to drink. God's actions are God's actions and we must be content to live with this mystery, rejoicing when He brings such immediate release, but also accepting it when He works in other ways. In either circumstance, we must simply trust in His love for us.

When a decision to change is coupled with faith in God, growth takes place. Rather than theorizing about this, let me simply share an experience out of my own life that illustrates what this marriage of repentance and faith can bring.

Not long ago, I became aware that my theoretical priorities were quite different from my actual ones. If anyone had asked me what I considered the most important commitments in my life I would have ranked my relationship to my family right up at the top. Yet, I came to realize, over the past year almost all my spare time had been devoted to work on my doctoral thesis. Even when I *was* spending time with my family, they often had the sense that I considered this a diversion from my real concern—the thesis. In order words, a good thing had subtly begun to dominate my life, throwing it out of balance.

My wife, in her usual perceptive way, saw what was happening and tried to point this out to me. At first I simply denied her insight. "No, I am not pre-occupied with my research. In fact I am spending a lot of time with all of you." Then I would compare how much more time I gave to the family than some of our friends.

This was to no avail. I came to realize that she was right. While it was true I spent more time with my kids than a lot of fathers, still it was nowhere near enough. So then I changed the nature of my defense (without realizing quite what I was doing). I tried to point out how crucial it was to finish this thesis and how deeply I was convinced that this was what God wanted me to do. (Both of which I still feel, incidentally.) So, if they could be patient just a while longer, I would finish the work and get back to a normal schedule. The problem was that the end of my research was not in sight and the kids were growing up.

This provoked a real crisis for me. I could not fit together both commitments. To finish the thesis (which I sensed was key in opening up new directions of ministry) I needed all the spare time I could find. But to be a real father and husband, I should be spending this same time with my family. I went through a very difficult period of questioning during which I was forced to look at a lot of my central assumptions in my life. It was not an enjoyable experience.

In the end, it was my faith which made it possible to decide to change my pattern of living. I suddenly came to see that the same God who called me to graduate work also called me to be a responsible part of my family. So in His mind no contradiction could exist. And while nothing could alter the growing up of my children (they needed me as a full-time father, *now*), in fact God could arrange for me to find another way to do the thesis. Perhaps I could get a fellowship which would free me for a while to study full time. I might inherit a lot of money from a distant (unknown) relative and accomplish the same end. Who knows? In any case, it was a renewed sense of God's sovereignty in my life that made it possible to let go of the thesis. If indeed He wanted me to finish this dissertation, He could and would provide the way. I could rest in that fact.

Not unexpectedly, this new sense of trust has had a freeing effect upon me. The research is no longer my burden alone. If I have read God's will accurately, I will be enabled to finish this work at some stage. For now, I can relax and enjoy my family. It is great to play baseball with the children, have a quiet cup of coffee with my wife, or to enjoy having friends over for dinner once again, without the sense that I should really be in my study at work. To my mind, this sense of rightness, this awareness of being "back on the right track," is the almost inevitable fruit of authentic repentance/faith responses.

We need to go on making such repentance/faith responses throughout our lives because of the nature of growth itself. We constantly need to undo the effects of evil and wrong choices in our lives by going back to the place we went astray, and starting again, this time on the right path. Our ability to repent, be forgiven, and start anew is the dynamic that enables on-going growth. C. S. Lewis expresses this well:

We are not living in a world where all roads are radii of a circle and where all, if followed long enough, will therefore draw gradually nearer and finally meet at the centre: rather in a world where every road, after a few miles, forks in two, and each of those into two again, and at each fork you must make a decision. Even on the biological level life is not like a pool but a tree. It does not move towards unity but away from it and the creatures grow further apart as they increase in perfection. Good, as it ripens, becomes continually more different not only from evil but from other good.

I do not think that all who choose wrong roads perish; but their rescue consists in being put back on the right road. A wrong sum can be put right: but only by going back till you find the error and working it afresh from that point, never by simply *going on*. Evil can be undone, but it cannot "develop" into good. Time does not heal it. The spell must be unwound, bit by bit, "with backward mutters of dissevering power"—or else not. It is still "either-or."[4]

It is this "going back till you find the error and working it afresh from that point" that makes all the difference. It is this capacity for *undoing the wrong* that makes it possible for us to grow toward wholeness. Otherwise, we would all be caught in a steady, inexorable descent into a hell in which we will have become the sum of all our wrong choices. If over the years we have continually given in to our bad temper, then that problem will more and more characterize who we are. If lust is our problem, the giving into a few small compromises at first can lead to more and larger compromises until there comes a surrender to lust. This chain can be broken, however, by repentance and faith. We can stop, be forgiven, and receive the power to walk in a new way. Repentance and faith are the keys not only to growth but to overcoming domination by all that threatens our true self.

▶ Inter Action

Repenting

I. Godly Grief: A Bible Study

Unlike Jesus, who spoke more often about repentance than He did about faith,[5] Saint Paul refers sparingly to repentance. In fact, he uses the word at only three places in his writings. However, in one of these passages (II Cor. 7), his discussion of repentance is so lucid that at least one commentator (Handley Moule) considers it the best description of repentance in all of Scripture. Since it is such a good treatment, and since it is clear that Paul is writing there to Christians (and not therefore discussing the initial repentance that leads to Christian conversion) we will study II Cor. 7:5-13a in some detail.

Before launching into a detailed study, however, it is important to sketch the background of this passage. Paul, it seems, was desperately worried about the Corinthian church, and with good cause. Apparently the church had begun to reflect in its own life the immorality for which the city of Corinth was so famous. Located at the point where virtually all the trade to and from Greece had to pass, Corinth had become wealthy, luxurious, and the scene of great debauchery. Typical of the atmosphere in Corinth was the great temple dedicated to Aphrodite, the goddess of love. One thousand priestesses were attached to the temple and were, in essence, sacred prostitutes. The very name "Corinth" had become synonymous in the ancient world with debauchery.

Paul had stayed longer in Corinth than in any other city except Ephesus. After he left Corinth and had gone to Ephesus, he heard that things were not going well in the Corinthian church. The church, it seems, had split into factions, each of which attached itself to a different teacher. Furthermore, the church members were taking each other to court, and asking non-Christians to decide on matters between Christians. If all this was not bad enough, apparently one of the church members was guilty of incest with his step-mother, a situation the church complacently accepted.

It is unclear exactly what took place, but it seems that Paul both visited Corinth and sent various letters in order to correct the situation. In II Cor. 7, where our study begins, Paul is anxiously awaiting news as to whether the problem has finally been resolved. He is so concerned that he has left Troas and taken a boat across to Macedonia to be nearer to Corinth so as to receive word all the sooner.

> For even when we came into Macedonia, our bodies had no rest but we were afflicted at every turn—fighting without and fear within. But God, who comforts the downcast, comforted us by the coming of Titus, and not

only by his coming but also by the comfort with which he was comforted in you, as he told us of your longing, your mourning, your zeal for me, so that I rejoiced still more. For even if I made you sorry with my letter, I do not regret it (though I did regret it), for I see that that letter grieved you, though only for a while. As it is, I rejoice, not because you were grieved, but because you were grieved into repenting; for you felt a godly grief, so that you suffered no loss through us. For godly grief produces a repentance that leads to salvation and brings no regret, but worldly grief produces death. For see what earnestness this godly grief has produced in you, what eagerness to clear yourselves, what indignation, what alarm, what longing, what zeal, what punishment! At every point you have proved yourselves guiltless in the matter. So although I wrote to you it was not on account of the one who did the wrong, nor on account of the one who suffered the wrong, but in order that your zeal for us might be revealed to you in the sight of God. Therefore we are comforted. (II Cor. 7:5-13a)

Using your notebook, answer the following questions as a means of analyzing the passage. Work through the questions in order, since the comments which follow depend upon your prior interaction with the text.

A. II Cor. 7:5ff is really a continuation of a previous passage which has been interrupted by a long parenthesis. Read II Cor. 1:15-2:13 to pick up the thread of Paul's thought.

B. Jot down the various words and phrases which describe Paul's physical and mental condition prior to Titus' arrival.

C. What brought relief to Paul?

D. Chart Paul's emotional ups and downs in this passage by listing in one column all the words and phrases that describe low points and in a second column, the words and phrases that describe his highs (see also verses 13b-16). What does this say about Paul as a man? How does this relate to Christian teaching that commends a constant smile as the mark of a true Christian?

E. Try to put yourself in Paul's place for a moment and feel with him the anguish he experienced over the disrupted fellowship with the Corinthians. Can you recall in your own experience how you felt when something came up between you and a close friend, and for one reason or another, you were unable to get together immediately to straighten it out? Can you remember the tension and the anxiety as you waited to see the outcome? This is what Paul felt, complicated by the long distances separating him from the Corinthians, and the fact of no convenient communications system. Try to feel his relief and joy then, when he found out that all was well again and their fellowship had been restored.

F. Why is it that Paul no longer regrets having written such a stern letter to the Corinthians? Why do you suppose he had had second thoughs about that letter?

G. What is the most frequently used word in verses 8-11 (in various verb forms and as a noun)?

H. Think about grief for a moment. What images does that word bring to mind? According to Paul, what is the role grief ought to play in our life?

I. According to Paul, what are the differences between "godly grief" and "worldly grief?"

J. One commentator has translated "godly grief" as "the pain God is allowed to guide." This sort of grief is set in contrast to "worldly grief." The basic difference between the two is that the former grief is referred back to God, the latter to ourselves. Godly grief is characterized by a real sorrow over our sins, whereas the sorrow of worldly grief comes mainly because our sin has been found out. If it had not been discovered, there would be no sorrow. Hence there is bitterness over being caught, rather than repentance (*i.e.,* the desire for change). This is why Paul says worldly grief produces death, while godly grief brings salvation. The one response leads to wholeness; the other to regret, self-pity, continued indulgence in the destructive action and hence to "death" in the broad sense of that word.

K. According to verse 11, what concrete change has taken place in the lives of the Corinthians, *i.e.,* what characterizes (and authenticates) their repentance? You might refer to a paraphrased version of II Corinthians to get a better sense of the meaning of each of these words and phrases in verse 11 since the Greek at this point is difficult to capture in a single English word.

L. Write an expanded paraphrase of verses 10 and 11 as a means of describing the nature of repentance.

M. The situation in Corinth was a bad one. The church was engaging in actions and displaying attitudes which Saint Paul knew would lead to destruction. In his role as spiritual father to the church, he points out the problems. In other words, Paul provided the necessary insight into the situation. Once the Corinthians were aware of the problem, the question was: How would they respond? Would they say "No" to the insight, rejecting Paul, getting mad over his "interference" and in essence going their own way? Or would they say "Yes," correct the problem and restore fellowship? Paul was torn apart awaiting the outcome. His despair, however, turns to overwhelming joy and pride in the Corinthians, when Titus returns with news of their repentance. They had been stung to the quick by Paul's entreaties. His insights had jarred them into awareness of the real situation, and this awareness in turn produced a godly grief that led to a zealous repentance. The end result was renewed fellowship between Paul and the church, and restoration of the church to its proper path. To my mind, this is an almost perfect example of what repentance is all about in the ongoing life of Christians.

N. Can you recall points in your life when you experienced this "godly grief" that Paul writes about? Describe this experience, noting particularly the impact of this grief upon your life. Can you recall instances when, in fact, what really bothered you was getting caught? Describe one of these experiences, thinking particularly about the outcome for you personally and for others around you.

O. Can you pinpoint an area in your life right now in which change is necessary? Define the problem. Note the direction in which change ought to take place. Think about what repentance and faith mean to you, right now, in that area.

II. Charting Our Christian Life

To complete your Pilgrimage Chart will take time and effort. I suggest you work on this little by little, while working through other chapters in *Pilgrimage*. Essentially, your aim should be to note the ups and downs of your life since that time when you consciously started following Jesus. Try to locate, first of all, significant periods in your Christian life. These periods may be characterized by a location; by a dominant influence (*e.g.*, a church or a course); by a change in life situation (*e.g.*, a new job, marriage); by a spiritual experience; by a crisis, etc. The work you have done in previous chapters will be a help to you.

Second, note the characteristics of each period of time: what new factors led into this period, what influences dominated that period, what you learned there, what you experienced, how you grew.

Third, be alert to what I call "mini-phases." It might be, for example, that it was as a Christian that you went through a period of time in which the nature of your commitment moved from ideas to people. Or, you may have gone through dark periods of doubt in which you asked the sort of questions other people ask during the Quest phase.

Finally, put all this together on your Pilgrimage Chart. Be particularly sensitive to where you now are in your pilgrimage.

Part III
Blockages to Growth

Still, they went on doggedly
blundering toward heaven.

   —Phyllis McGinley, *Saint-Watching*

9 "Fighting Without": External Impediments to Christian Growth

The theory is that once we become a Christian the battle is over. We have broken through the jungle of tangled ideas and incomplete truths and stumbled into the sunlit clearing where for the first time we see what life is all about. From then on, to mix my metaphors even further, it is clear sailing. Oh sure, there may be problems along the way, but by and large, life as a Christian is just a bowl of cherries.

This, as I say, is the theory (at least for some people). It never works out that way in practice (which causes one to wonder why the myth of "Come to Christ and all will be well" is still propagated). The Christian life is not an unending foretaste of eternal bliss. In fact, we may find that by becoming Christ's followers we are introduced to a whole host of new problems (like caring for the hungry, working for justice, suffering the consequences of honesty, and all those other things that come when we take Jesus' view of the world seriously). The battle, it seems, has simply moved to a new front.

Not only that, we also find that our growth as Christians is not as automatic and straightforward as we assumed. We have our ups but we also have our downs. We experience moments of stunning insight but shortly thereafter our blindness re-asserts itself. We find that our enthusiasm is balanced by our lethargy. But nonetheless, we generally do keep moving—albeit by fits and starts.

However, there do come those points when our growth is seriously impeded. It isn't a matter any longer of a temporary detour. Rather, it is as if a roadblock had been thrown across our path. We are stopped dead, stalled in our tracks.

This is what the next two chapters are all about—roadblocks that seriously impede our Christian growth. I want to identify some of those roadblocks and then discuss strategies for circumventing them so as to get going again on our pilgrimage. In this chapter my intention is to look at external impediments to growth, that is, at those factors in our environment which inhibit growth. Specifically, I will examine the way *institutions* can obstruct growth and then, briefly, the way *difficult circumstances* affect our Christian life. In the next chapter the focus will be in the other direction, *i.e.*, on the inner doubts and fears that are often the biggest obstacles to change.

Institutions

I first met Jack in 1962 when he was a student at the Detroit Bible Institute. Our encounter then was brief. However, five years later, Jack wrote me. He was by then in the import-export business and needed some information about trade conditions in South Africa. As it turned out, my family and I were just about to leave South Africa on furlough so I suggested that rather than trying to answer all his questions via a letter, we ought to meet and talk when I returned to the States.

A month later we had lunch together. I can remember being immediately impressed by Jack. He was one of those rare individuals who was brimming with energy and running over with ideas. We spent nearly three hours talking non-stop.

Throughout our conversation I kept thinking how incredible it would be if all Jack's creative energy were ever channeled into the work of the church. God had given him some very special gifts.

Yet, as it turned out, this was the one area where Jack had a difficult time relating. It seems that he had grown up in a very strict church and while he had never left his commitment to Christ, he had left the church—after years of total involvement. He did so because he could no longer live with the rigid codes imposed upon church members with little more than prejudice to justify them. Nor could he tolerate any longer the blind spots in the church's vision. He saw and knew that their stand on racial issues, on politics, and even on theology contained glaring inconsistencies. Most of all, he could not stand the boredom. He might have tolerated the rest if he were learning and growing, but the church had long since stopped speaking to his needs.

Jack's situation, however, was not all that unusual, and generally a person like him would simply move to a different church. But this proved to be impossible for Jack. He had been told for so long that this one particular church was virtually the only "true" church and that all others were heretical, that he had come to feel that his choice was to go to that church or no church at all. So he simply dropped out of the church. This was not an easy decision. Jack had meaningful spiritual commitments.

Now he no longer had a place to which he could turn to be affirmed in them.

The tragedy of all this lies not only in Jack's sense of spiritual frustration but in the loss of his immensely creative input to the ongoing work of the church. He had so much to give and no medium through which to express it.

Jack's experience with this one church is not unique. Christian institutions, it seems, are a mixed blessing. On the one hand, they provide invaluable input to our spiritual lives. Worship, teaching, and fellowship are all vital ingredients to Christian growth. Furthermore, these institutions provide the means whereby we can express our Christian faith in service to others. On the other hand, churches and other Christian groups can become for us major impediments to our growth as Christians. We all know this to be true though we often do not like to admit it—because none of us likes to see the church failing to be the Church in all its power and glory. Yet the simple fact remains: many Christians are harmed, not helped, by the church to which they belong.

It is not easy to know what a person ought to do when he begins to feel alienated from the church he is attending. The first attempt should always be to try to work through the difficulty whether it is stagnation, disillusionment, or a breakdown in interpersonal relationships. After all, it seems from the New Testament that broken relationships are the norm (which is why so much is said about how to repair them). Dietrich Bonhoeffer goes a step further by suggesting that before real Christian community can even develop, a group must experience "shattering."

> Innumerable times a whole Christian community has broken down because it had sprung from a wish dream. The serious Christian, set down for the first time in a Christian community, is likely to bring with him a very definite idea of what Christian life together should be and try to realize it. But God's grace speedily shatters such dreams. Just as surely God desires to lead us to a knowledge of genuine Christian fellowship, so surely must we be overwhelmed by a great general disillusionment with others, with Christians in general, and, if we are fortunate, with ourselves.
>
> By sheer grace God will not permit us to live even for a brief period in a dream world. He does not abandon us to those rapturous experiences and lofty moods that come over us like a dream. God is not a God of the emotions but the God of truth. Only that fellowship which faces such disillusionment, with all its unhappy and ugly aspects, begins to be what it should be in God's sight, begins to grasp in faith the promise that is given to it. The sooner this shock of disillusionment comes to an individual and to a community the better for both. A community which cannot bear and cannot survive such a crisis, which insists upon keeping its illusion when it should be shattered, permanently loses in that moment the promise of Christian community. Sooner or later it will collapse. Every human wish dream that is injected into the Christian community is a hindrance to genuine community and must be banished if genuine community is to survive.[1]

So perhaps our calling is to stay right where we are and seek to bring about change in that place. Perhaps our insights, creativity, or just our openness will be the channel which God uses to breathe new life into that particular body.

It is not easy to be the one who challenges the *status quo*. There is a price to be paid for that sort of stance. You will be misunderstood, avoided, misquoted, and rejected and none of these are enjoyable experiences. Yet time and again, down through the ages, God has called upon men and women, in big ways and in small, to be true to what they know is right despite the opposition they have to face. They may never see any change (although it is often true that more is happening than meets the eye). But still they are called upon to *be* what God has made them to be and to stand for what they have seen is true.

However, there is a limit to how long a person is able to (or should) remain in a non-supportive situation. Limits vary from person to person. But one thing is clear. When our attitude begins to shift from love and tolerance to hostility and bitterness, it is time to leave. As long as you can continue to support the aims of the group and retain a basic love and respect for the people in it (despite what appears to be a lot of nonsense at times on their part), your voice can be a creative one. When this support and acceptance begins to waver, it is time to ask whether you ought to leave.

But leaving a group is not easy either. There will always be good friends that you will miss. There will be fond memories that are hard to leave behind. There will be so much of yourself that has been poured into a place that you are loathe to give it all up. Then, too, there will be the fear of the unknown. After all, even though the situation has become difficult, still you understand it, while moving is always a step in the dark. Yet, for all this, there still comes that point when to stay is to become destructive to others as well as to yourself.

How then does one leave a group? Do you simply stop attending? It is interesting to look at the different ways people leave groups.

One friend had been active in his church for years. As a result, he eventually was elected to the ruling body. The custom in the church was for each leader to go on sabbatical after a certain number of years in order to gain a new perspective and so be refreshed for further service. My friend took his sabbatical quite seriously. He withdrew from all his commitments at the church. He even stopped attending the services regularly. At the end of the year he simply did not return. He had found in his time away that not only was the church no longer really meeting his spiritual needs, but that he personally had reached a point where the contributions he could make would not be seen as useful.

I know one family that has *psychologically* left their church. After years and years of enthusiastic but futile effort aimed at moving the church towards new life and concern, they have simply given up. They are unable to face any more hostility. They still live in the neighborhood.

They attend the church occasionally and still relate to their friends there. But they no longer offer any input.

This situation is not uncommon. Many people retain a nominal interest in their church (e.g., they attend the morning service), but their real enthusiasm is reserved for other areas of Christian service and fellowship such as small-group Bible studies, political activity on behalf of the underprivileged, involvement in the lives of teenagers, or whatever. If we do come to the point that we decide we must leave a group it is important to give reasons. Otherwise a lot of relationships are left dangling and misunderstanding is sure to result. Not only that, if we leave silently, we deprive the community of the insights which have led to our departure. People may not agree with our understanding of the situation but at least they should be made aware of the problem. One friend wrote a long letter to the church he left, detailing his reasons—not in a spirit of antagonism but out of concern. Apart from any benefit his insights might have been to the church, he felt that he personally needed to write such a letter. Until he did so, the whole situation was unresolved and troubling to him.

The danger in this is that the protest can become so vociferous that battle lines are drawn up and people start "taking sides." When this happens there is a real question as to whether creative growth can take place. Yet there are times when it is impossible to be silent—despite the potential disruption that might be created—because it is so evident that the church is simply not facing the issues. These frustrations in the face of what appears to be willful blindness can drive a person to try to "force" others to see by being as public and as vocal as possible.

There is another angle to all this. Some individuals, particularly younger people, have become so wary of any institution that they never really get involved. They float from church to church as spiritual vagabonds. To be sure, they never have to face the agony of leaving. People are hardly aware they have been there. But they pay a big price for this non-involvement. Whole avenues of growth are cut off to them because they lack the sustenance of a body.

This has implications for us if we do have to leave a group. The danger is that we will become one of these vagabonds. So, in leaving a group, it is important to leave *for something else*. We all need to be part of a fellowshipping group—be it a church or just a small group of like-minded Christians. We cannot exist in a creative and useful way as Christians when we are surrounded by a spiritual vacuum. We do need others in order to learn and grow. We need others to love and support us; and in turn, we need a body in which to exercise our particular spiritual gifts. We need a group through which to express our Christian concern for the needs of the world.

In all of this what I am trying to say is that it is not necessarily a bad thing to leave a particular church. I think that all too often we have been conditioned to believe, as Jack did, that our only options are staying in a particular church or not going to any church at all. In fact, it seems more and more true that different churches fill different needs at different points in our lives. And that to grow, at times we must move on to a new environment where we will flourish.

The same is true of the various para-church groups that exist—those interdenominational bodies that function independently from the church—like Young Life, the Full-Gospel Businessmen's Fellowship, and the Gideons. All that I have said thus far about churches applies equally well to these sorts of groups, including the need, at times, to leave them and move on.

My own life has had its share of "moving on." As a teenager, two groups were immensely valuable to me—my church and Youth For Christ. When I left Detroit and went away to college (thus in effect severing the ties) I joined an Inter-Varsity Christian Fellowship group and for the next four years profited enormously from its ministry. Again, my tie with IVCF was severed by moving, this time from college on the East Coast to Seminary on the West Coast (though I did serve two more years as part-time IVCF Staff). At this point, the most important force in my spiritual growth was a small, informal group of students interested in urban evangelism in Africa (which later developed into a mission work with which I served).

As I look back on these and the other groups of which I have been a part, several things strike me. First, certain groups were right for me at certain times in my pilgrimage. But these same groups, at a different point, would have had a negative influence. Take the Youth for Christ group in High School, for example. I really enjoyed that group at the time—with its enthusiasm, its Bible memory quizes, its high-powered evangelism, and its large rallies. It fitted where I was in my growth and appealed to the sort of person I was then. Later on, as my views of evangelism changed, as I grew wary of high pressure ways of presenting Christianity, and as my enthusiasm for large meetings wanned, YFC would not have been a good experience for me (as it was not everyone's cup of tea even while I was a member).

Second, to stay on in a group beyond the time it is meaningful is often very unfortunate. When it has become clear that the differences in the group are too great to be resolved (this presupposes substantial effort to work through the issues); or when it has become evident that in staying you are compromising your own integrity; then you must leave, and quickly. To prolong a situation that has become destructive is to court disaster.

Third, no one group has a corner on truth. This seems so obvious that it hardly needs stating, but I have been in at least one group (and know of others) in which this was the tacit assumption on the part of all the members. In the group I belonged to, we really felt that we had superior insights and ways of doing things. The result was a certain arrogance, a disdain for other groups (particularly those that were similar in purpose to ours), and an inability to learn from others. This, of course, makes growth impossible, either for the group or for individuals within it. On the other hand, while no group sees everything clearly, each group does have particular emphases and insights which make it unique and give it a reason for being—at least in its own eyes. We should recognize these strengths and learn all we can from them. The time may come when we move on, so while we are part of the group we should avail ourselves of the special thing that is to be learned.

Fourth, it serves no creative purpose to criticize endlessly other groups. Of course they have their weaknesses and blindnesses. So do all groups. So does each one of us. This is not to say that we should close our eyes to such weaknesses, or stop trying to help those in the group to see more clearly. But there is a difference between this sort of creative input and the castigation of which we are all too often guilty.

Fifth, it is quite possible over a period of time to accumulate a series of commitments to various groups which we retain by force of habit long after the groups have ceased to be meaningful to us or we to them. Several years ago, it became clear to me that this was my situation. I had been led to accept a new commitment which required all of my spare time and so had to drop out of various groups. When I did so, I realized that I was not at all unhappy to be leaving. In fact, I was glad for the excuse to resign. It was not that I had lost my confidence in the groups, nor that I was having difficulty relating to the people there. It was simply that my needs and my ability to give had changed. This became clear when I started the new project and experienced a great flow of creative energy. I felt that I was learning again and that I was using my God-given gifts in the way they should be used. Just recently I came across a passage in a book by John Gardner which expresses what I had experienced.

> It is not unusual to find that the major changes in life—marriage, a move to a new city, a change of jobs or a national emergency—break the patterns of our lives and reveal to us quite suddenly how much we had been imprisoned by the comfortable web we had woven around ourselves. Unlike the jailbird, we don't know that we've been imprisoned until after we've broken out.[2]

It is not easy to decide to leave a group when you still feel good about it. This is quite different from leaving because you can no longer identify with a group's aims. Yet, in both cases, it may be the response of faith to move on to new commitments. To learn the ability to say "No" is often a spiritual breakthrough of major significance.

This talk about leaving churches and other Christian groups scares a lot of people, especially those who have to look after the running of such institutions. And not without reason. It is impossible to build a meaningful community if people run off to new groups the minute something displeases them. True fellowship is often wrought *as a result* of shared trials and difficulties.

There is an added danger peculiar to the American scene. We are a people that like winners. And we flock to a place that we sense is "successful." Hence the exodus of people from small, struggling churches to the one huge church in town with the large staff, big budget, and multi-faceted programs. For the same reason, people flock to every new "spiritual leader" who promises a more fulfilling life.

Somewhere there must be a balance between the needs of the individual and the needs of the institution. I suspect that part of the answer lies in the ability of an *institution* to grow and develop in the same way that a Christian must grow and develop. This does not always happen. In fact, there seem to be two basic kinds of institutions: those that are static and those that are developing. The first kind are often the product of a single bright idea which gets turned into an organization. Someone says, "Hey, we could evangelize this town by dropping tracts from a blimp into everyone's backyard," and hence the Gospel Blimp Ministry is formed.[3] A charismatic leader then persuades a group of (wealthy) businessmen to back his ideas. An office is secured, a blimp and hangar rented, tracts are purchased, staff is trained, and the ministry is launched (literally). At this point, the institution faces a choice. It can do its job of dropping tracts in backyards year in and year out, until it becomes a well-known and respected ministry which people assume has always existed. Or it can face the much more perilous option of constant openness to the guidance of God in its evolution, developing perhaps into a multi-facted evangelistic ministry, or into a ministry to airport personnel or perhaps to trash collectors. Or even, perish the thought, it might dissolve itself after a few years when the task it set out to accomplish is completed. (Of course, the fundamental question which never seems to get asked by such para-church ministries is whether they even ought to exist in the first place—but that is not the subject of this chapter!)

It is not simply specialized groups that risk the possibility of becoming static. Churches, too, can easily come to the point where they simply strive to maintain the *status quo*. The worship services are always the same. The groups in the church never change but go on functioning in identical fashion year after year; the same types of programs are run year in and year out. The problem is that all too often the growth needs of individual members have developed past the point where these never-changing groups can meet them.

The other possibility is for a church (or group) to seek consciously to grow and change. It seems to me that these are the sorts of institutions which are able to retain membership over a long period of time. The reason is clear. Individual and institutional growth parallel one another and there is great cross-fertilization. What the institution is learning is of significance for the individual, and likewise the individual's on-going discoveries fuel the instutition's growth.

This is not the place to get into the whole question of church renewal. Suffice it to say that vital, growing churches do exist, within which individuals are finding exactly the sort of input they need to keep on growing. There is ample literature describing such churches and the reasons for their dynamism.

Difficult Circumstances

Circumstances, as well as institutions, can create roadblocks to growth. We are all aware of the fact that from time to time we find ourselves, through no fault of our own, in a situation that makes Christian growth exceedingly difficult.

Sometimes the problem is a lack of time. Of necessity we get involved in a task that demands our full attention so that we have little time left for eating and sleeping much less for quiet meditation and theological reflection. Every young mother knows what this is all about.

Perhaps it is our job that consumes all our energy. Not all that long ago, there were large numbers of workers in the United States who labored long hours at exhausting jobs in order to produce a meager income. While such killing hours are no longer the norm in the United States, they remain so in certain other countries. In South Africa, for example, it is not uncommon for a servant to be asked to work from 6:45 a.m. to 8:30 p.m. six days a week (with Saturday afternoon off) and then from 6:45 a.m. to 2:00 p.m. on Sunday—all this for a wage well below the breadline.

Simone Weil, that strange French mystic, discovered for herself how crippling to the soul routine and tedious production jobs can be. In her passionate identification with the poor of the world, she left her teaching post—for which her brilliance had fitted her ideally—and chose instead to labor on farms and in factories. As she reported in her journals, she was appalled at her inability to work and think at the same time. The nature of the 'output' that was demanded left neither time nor energy for creativity, and she became deeply depressed over the servitude of the worker to the mechanism of his job.

In such circumstances, it is exceedingly difficult to do much else but survive. There is no time for fellowship and worship much less for serious study and involvement in acts of Christian charity.

However, unrelenting labor and over-filled schedules are not the only circumstances that inhibit our potential for growth. Illness, isolation, and personal turmoil can also affect our pilgrimage. Illness is an obvious problem. A throbbing pain in the abdomen draws to itself all our concentration. We have little attention to turn in other directions. Personal turmoil has the same effect. When we are fighting for the very survival of our personality, we have little energy left over for other considerations. Isolation is a different sort of problem. In this case it is not that we are so flooded with input that we can scarcely lift our head to give thought to anything else. It is quite the opposite. In our aloneness we are starved for stimulation of some sort, without which we eventually lose our motivation. All labor seems pointless when we are alone in our own world.

These are but a few of the circumstances which make growth difficult. The list could go on for pages. But all the circumstances share one thing in common. They demand an excessive amount of our concentration and energy so that we have few resources left over for growth. Survival, not wholeness, is the issue we face.

What then can we do when we find ourselves caught in a difficult situation? Often our first response is to seek a way out. We get medical treatment; we look for another job; we try to make friends. A second response is to try to work through the difficulty. We seek counseling; we learn to handle our pain; we develop a perspective that will enable us to cope.

The right perspective is crucial. For one thing, it is very important to be aware that circumstances are often beyond our control. We did not create them. We cannot control them. So it is not very profitable to spend a lot of time fretting over what a rotten deal we have.

Second, a lot of difficult situations will, in time, come to an end. Our circumstances will not always be the same. Infants do grow up, giving mother free time once again. Illnesses can be treated.

Third, we can learn, given time, how to cope better in demanding situations. We can learn to use our free moments creatively. We can learn, as did Brother Lawrence, to wash dishes and simultaneously live in God's presence. We can also come to see that the very circumstances we have found inhibiting may also be capable of creating growth. Washing dishes can become a means of grace. Active participation in the development of your child is as growth-producing as meditation. Out of difficult circumstances, valuable lessons can emerge. We do learn things we would not have known had the circumstances been easier. As a result of living in an isolated region, for example, we learn to cherish friendship in a new way. Or perhaps through a difficult relationship we grow aware of our need for God's help in order to love. In other words, difficult circumstances are not invariably a hindrance to growth. They can be a source of new insight and development. This I take to be one of the meanings of Romans 8:28: ". . . all things work together for good to them that love God." Our attitude seems to be the key. Do we fight, despise and chafe under what we cannot change, or do we accept it (without necessarily liking it) and learn from it?

No difficulty is pleasant—no matter how instructive it may turn out to be. And Christianity is not a masochistic religion that encourages its followers to pursue pain. Rather, our example is Jesus, the Suffering Servant, who *endured,* and out of His pain came salvation. If we can avoid difficult circumstances, well and good. If not, then we may have to shift for a time from growth to defense. The pilgrim, if anyone, ought to be able to make this sort of adjustment. One of the marks of a healthy personality (and this is what the pilgrim is in the process of developing) is flexibility in meeting new circumstances. Our world, like it or not, is the sort of place in which everyone sooner or later will face adverse circumstances. This is not a pleasant fact. It is simply a fact.

▶ Inter Action

Groups

I. The Past

On a sheet of paper, make three columns (as shown in the example below). Then try to recall all the Christian groups to which you have belonged, but of which you are no longer a part. Include in this list the local churches you attended, the para-church groups you belonged to, and even the informal groups which you joined. List sub-groups as well (*e.g.,* the Men's Fellowship in the church). You might even want to list secular groups, especially if they were significant in your growth.

One by one, put down the dates you were active in a particular group, the name of the group, and then, in a phrase or two, the characteristics of that group as well as its significance for you.

Example:

Dates	Group	Characteristics and Significance
1953-1961	"Local" Church	—a very orthodox church
		—gained initial Christian insights here
	a) Youth Group	—very active, lots of meetings, picnics, etc.; fairly closed
	—exec. committee	—learned about planning programs; discovered need to make meetings interesting as well as informative
	b) Sunday School Class	—dull and badly taught, with a few exceptions
1953-54	Youth for Christ Club	
1954	Inner City Evangelism Group	

Next, isolate what you consider the *worst* group experience you had. What made it so? How did you cope? What lessons did you learn?

Which was the *best* group experience? Why? What did you learn from this group? Why did you leave the group?

Think about how you left each group. Were there any particularly bad experiences in leaving? Why?

II. The Present

Make a similar list for the groups to which you currently belong. In addition, for each group list: 1) your level of involvement; 2) the ways you contribute; 3) what you gain; 4) how you feel about the group.

Think about your group participation in the context of your total Christian life. How are the groups contributing to your growth? Are any impeding it? How can you gain or give more to the groups?

III. The Future

This is a chance for you to use your creative imagination. The aim of this part of the exercise is for you to design the "ideal" group.

First, think about where you are now as a person. What are your needs in terms of growth? Is there a specific question which is troubling you and into which you would like more insight? Are you facing relational problems? Career/life-direction problems? Are you frustrated at your inability to use the gifts of ministry which God has given you? Do you long for fellowship of the sort that is characterized by honest sharing, love, and burden-bearing? In as specific a way as possible, catalogue the experiences you crave.

Second, design a group that could meet these needs. What sort of people would you like in it? How could it be structured? How could it function? What would be its purpose(s)? What size should it be? What kinds of inputs would be useful? How would it be led? How would disagreement within the group be handled?

Let your imagination loose. List all the ideas that come to you. Don't reject any, no matter how far-fetched they might be. In fact, just jot down all your ideas as they come to you. Then gradually shape them into a concrete form. Complete this work before you go on to read the next paragraph.

I assume you now have the design in hand for your model group. Now think about what it would take to implement your ideas. Obviously you will not be able to put into effect every aspect of your plan (*e.g.*, I doubt if Bruce Larson and Keith Miller will be able to lead the group). But other aspects will be practical. In fact, there is probably a core to your ideas that could be implemented. Consider carefully whether you ought not to pursue these ideas—in the context of your church or some other group, or on your own. Remember, what you crave, others will also crave. Perhaps, just perhaps, the next step for you in your pilgrimage will be the creation of a group that will meet not only your needs but also those of others.

10 "Fear Within . . .": Internal Obstacles to Growth

It should be clear by now that the pilgrim is not without problems. As Saint Paul expressed it, there is "fighting without and fear within." In the previous chapter, attention was directed to some of the "fighting without." Now the focus shifts to "fear within"—to those inner problems which haunt and distract us and so block our growth.

Fear

Fear, as everyone knows, is an emotion. Sometimes it is readily identifiable: it is what we feel when we are swimming in water much too deep for our ability and we start to get a cramp. At other times, it is not so easy to identify. We meet a new person at a party, and find he is also interested in Christianity, but from quite a different perspective. He feels all religions, and especially Christianity, are a lot of nonsense. He is clever, witty, terribly well informed, and able to argue persuasively. After an hour of conversation we begin to wonder if he really is right and we have been living with falsehoods. "No," we tell ourselves, "he couldn't be right." But inside we are shaken. This, too, is fear . . . fear of what that other person stands for, fear of his ideas, fear that we *may* be wrong, fear that we will be made to look foolish because we can't express our beliefs very well; and this fear is every bit as real as the fear of physical danger.

No one likes fear. It is an emotion we go to great lengths to avoid. The next time we go swimming we are careful not to venture into deep water. At the next party we studiously avoid our debunking friend. And herein lies the problem. Fear causes us to shy away from certain situations, and while this makes sense when it comes to physical danger, it can be crippling to our growth. Fear causes us to avoid the very situations which could provoke us to new growth.

Fear is a marvellous warning system. It tips us off to the fact that we are getting into a dangerous situation. Hence it is an emotion vital to our very survival—both physically and psychologically. Yet there are times when we must note our fear, and then continue on into the situation anyway. We are afraid of deep water and yet there is a child out there who is drowning. Our ability to overcome our fear for the sake of a higher purpose is at the very heart of our "humanness."

What is true in facing physical danger is also true of psychologically threatening situations. At times, in order to grow, we must put aside our fear and face the threat. Otherwise we will be bound by our fear. We will never really know what, if anything, is behind the threat. A whole area of growth and inquiry will be off limits to us as a result of our fear.

I am thinking of situations such as the first time I had to take part in a debate at a university during a Christian mission. I did not know what to expect, was unsure whether I could answer the questions, and in general was terribly ill at ease. I was afraid to put myself in a situation where I could get blasted. In any case, having little choice, I went ahead with the meeting and had a marvellous time. I found that behind the phantom of "hostile university intellectuals" was nothing more than a group of men and women who were also struggling to know what life was all about and were genuinely grateful for any new input. Their questions were generally sincere, and I found I could handle the few that were barbed. The outcome of all this was a sense of new freedom in my ministry at universities. Had I not plunged ahead despite my fears, I would have remained uneasy in university situations and not nearly as effective as I could have been. My fear would have kept me from seeing behind the myth of the "hostile university environment."

There will come those times for each of us when in order to grow we have to face squarely a situation from which we would prefer to run. It may involve, for example, confronting the argument of those who say Christianity is untrue, such as the person at the party. Our temptation is simply to write off the guy with a label of some sort: "He's just an arrogant pipsqueak who thinks he knows more than he does." Or we may try to put the whole encounter out of our mind, pretending that people like that really don't exist. Either of these responses signals a retreat back into the security of our boundaries, without having learned anything from the encounter. This is the settler mentality at work again.

We pay a price for such a retreat. No matter how hard we try we will probably not be able to forget what has been said, or at least, forget that there are people who think they can disprove Christianity. Hence we will be fearful. "What if Christianity is untrue?" we ask ourselves in our dark moments.

How much better to face the issue squarely for what it is. Once we do this we often find that the problem is not nearly as overwhelming as we had imagined. We also find that as Christians we have tremendous resources available to us. We have the thinking of some of the finest minds in history to which we can refer. (We can be pretty sure that the problems raised at a party are not new.) We have all the people within the Christian community to whom we can turn for help and support. In other words, what we feared might cause us to "lose our faith" turns out instead to be a tremendous opportunity for learning and growth. But this could never have come about if our constant posture is that of retreat and defense.

Not all fear is rooted in concrete situations. At times it is future possibilities that worry us. There are, for example, the "what if" fears which assail us late at night: what if I get sick and can't work, how will I feed the family; what if my son falls out of a second story window; what if . . . and on it goes. "What if" fears can, of course, provoke us to necessary action: we take out disability insurance or we put up storm windows on the second floor. But all too often they simply eat away at us, making us anxious and uneasy.

To overcome such fears all we have to do at times is to sit down and ask ourselves: "O.K., what is it that I am afraid of?" and then list as precisely as possible the exact nature of the fear. Often we will find that this very process of identification has itself greatly lessened our fear. We see that what we feared is not very real or not very probable. Or we find that we could handle the problem if it ever came up; or we devise ways to prevent this from ever being a problem. It is important to remember that there are the sorts of fears that arise from situations which *might* take place, not from situations that have already taken place (and in which we do have to choose to avoid or to face the problem). Nevertheless, this fear of what might be is very real and can be very inhibiting by virtue of the way it preoccupies us.

Sometimes we are unable to overcome these irrational fears by ourselves. This is the point at which we ought to seek professional help. Certain fears simply cannot be dealt with except by a trained counselor or psychiatrist.

Having said all this about the need to face our fears and overcome them rather than give into the desire to avoid the issue, it is now necessary to add that there are those times when we simply do not have the resources to handle a given situation, and the counsel of wisdom is to flee. Perhaps you are a new Christian. You have just discovered who Jesus is and have joyously begun to follow Him. A friend invites you to attend a weekend conference run by the Unification Church. You have heard a little about this new movement. It seems to be Christian, but then, doesn't Dr. Sun Moon claim to be greater than Jesus Himself, and in fact, an incarnation of God? You are wary, but who knows, it might be a good place to share about your discovery of Jesus. Yet, when all is said and done, you still do not feel comfortable about going.

This is a situation in which avoidance is probably in order. The new

Christian simply does not have the background to sort out what is Christian, much less the ability to interact at any depth with the Moon children. At best, he would come away from the weekend confused and troubled. Later on, after he has matured in his understanding and experience, he could handle such input. But not now.

The best way to know whether we ought to avoid or face an issue is to ask ourselves: where is the cutting edge of my growth right now? If indeed, the point corresponds with the threatening situation, then we probably ought to overcome our fear and plunge in. If not, there is always another more opportune day when the situation will be growth-producing for us and not simply threatening. The pilgrim's journey is slow and deliberate.

Fear can inhibit our growth in many different ways. We fear mistakes, so we never try to do anything new. You won't find us volunteering to help run a Junior High Retreat. We'd probably just mess it up. And so we are never able to explore new areas in which we might well have God-given but undeveloped skills.

Then there is the fear of other's opinions. This is a powerful deterrent to investigating anything outside the consensus of our group. This fear is related to the fear of disrupting fellowship. We know that our exploration of certain areas will be misunderstood by some and will affect our relationship with them. And people may, in fact, cut us off because of what they view as our un-Christian behavior or opinion. We have become a threat to them—arousing their own fears much as did the man at the party in my first illustration. If we are not cut off from fellowship, then we are subjected to great pressure.

We have to be aware of these reactions. And, I have come to believe, there are times when it is more important for us to give up a certain area of behavior or inquiry, than to disturb others who cannot handle our actions. But again, the decision to refrain or persist is a personal one, directly related to the path along which God is leading us. Either response could be growth-producing.

When it comes right down to it, a number of our fears relate to the whole question of doubt. Because aligning ourselves with God's truth is so very important to us as Christians, we all carry with us (or should) a fear of leaving what is true for the sake of what is not. This fear of counterfeit ideas is very deep. A problem develops when this fear causes us to avoid any new or threatening idea; when we come to feel that questioning itself invariably leads to disbelief. Since it is vital to ask questions in order to grow as Christians, and since this fear of questions is so pervasive, it is necessary to look at this subject in some detail.

The Fear of Doubting

I once spent six weeks in Uganda during which time I lived on a lovely tea plantation some miles outside Kampala, the capital. This tea plantation was the center in that area of the so-called Revival Movement. I had heard a lot about this movement, how it had revolutionized the relationships between the missionaries and the local Christians; how it had resulted in strong leadership in the church; how the Revival Christians were eagerly sought by employers because they were so honest, etc. As such I was eager to learn all I could. So I went about questioning everyone in sight, trying to get a grasp on the distinctives of the movement. In particular I had long conversations with my hostess, a gracious English lady. One day in the course of our discussion, she said to me (in the characteristically honest fashion of Revival Christians) that she felt I spent too much time asking questions when in fact what I really needed to do was simply "believe."

At the time I was bothered a bit by this rejoinder. I really did want to learn all I could about the Revival and this was the reason for my questions. Before I could incorporate its unique insights into my own Christian life, I had to understand how they fitted into a traditional Christian framework—so I was baffled by her comment. Now, I think I understand better what she was concerned about. She felt, as do many other people, that doubt will lead us away from truth—and that questioning is, in essence, equivalent to doubt. She was genuinely concerned for me that I not lose my way in a labyrinth of questions.

Of course, there is an element of truth to such concern. Questioning can lead to doubt which in turn can lead to disbelief. However, questioning can also lead to growth and new insight. This, then, is the problem. How do we distinguish between these two types of questions? I think the answer will become evident as we look at the nature of belief and doubt; and at the role questioning plays in our life.

First, it is necessary to be quite clear about why it is that we must ask questions if we are to grow as Christians. The fundamental reason, quite simply, is that none of us understands everything perfectly. By virtue of the Fall, our very ability to comprehend what is true is limited. We are simply not able to see all the facets of a particular truth, nor are we able to inter-relate what we do see with all the other issues that bear upon it. This is a built-in limitation which all human beings share, rendering each of us incapable of complete understanding. Hence in order to grow we must constantly seek to understand things better, and this will involve ongoing questioning.

Knowing this limitation in our understanding ought to make us far less anxious about our beliefs. Of course we are going to misunderstand some things. We cannot help doing so. But this is what growth is all about: attempting to clarify and to comprehend ever more accurately what is really true.

This ought to warn us, too, about the pronouncements of other people. Sometimes we seem to fall into the trap of considering certain other people's viewpoints as virtually infallible. We recognize our own limitations but forget that everyone else has limitations, too. So if a well-known leader says something (or, for that matter, our neighbor with a

Ph.D), then we believe it. It is almost as if our blind acceptance of the word of an authority figure somehow compensates for our personal inability to see clearly.

Authority figures can be major stumbling blocks in our growth. While it is true that they may offer to us new insights which are crucial for our growth, all too often these insights come as part of a total package and we are led to believe that we have got to accept the whole system or nothing at all. Consequently we can become enslaved to the ideas of one teacher. The result of this is that our growth becomes limited to the radius of his particular insights.

There is another implication that arises from the fact that our understanding is flawed—we will never be completely free from doubt. We will never be able to know with absolute and total certainty that all we believe is without error. Only a fool can claim that he sees everything clearly and hence does not need to doubt. The rest of us, alas, are in a much more tenuous situation. There are certain things of which we are quite certain, others we are certain are wrong, while we are unsure about all the rest.

Hence doubt is not necessarily wrong. It is simply a fact of life. In fact, it seems to be true that even within our belief there is doubt! The father of the epileptic boy cried out to Jesus: "I believe; help my unbelief!" (Mark 9:24). It is not simply a matter of believing something or not believing it. Often we do believe, but still there are unresolved questions. But these questions, these doubts, are not inherently bad. In fact, it is out of our struggle to resolve them that we gain new and totally unexpected insights. Many of our deepest convictions develop as a result of our attempts to come to grips with inner doubts. The point where faith and doubt mingle can be the source of rich new growth.

But what does this say about belief if it can contain doubt as part of it? Apart from anything else, it is an indication that belief itself can grow and develop. We believe, but we can come to believe even more or at a new depth. There is an interesting story at the end of John 4 which illustrates this. An official from Capernaum had come to Jesus because his child was dying. Jesus was in Cana at the time and the official begged Him to journey back to Capernaum with him in order to heal his child. Instead, Jesus simply said: "Go, your son will live." According to John, "The man believed the word that Jesus spoke to him and went on his way." In other words, the man's belief was so strong that he stopped begging Jesus to come home with him and simply departed, trusting that his son would be well. Yet in verse 53, after he hears from his servant that his child is indeed alive, John reports: "He (the man) himself believed, and all his household." But he had already believed, hadn't he? Notice, however, his original belief was that Jesus had healed his son. Yet after his servant verified this, the man no longer needed to believe. He now *knew* it to be true. This new response of belief, therefore, was a different, deeper sort. Now he believed *in* Jesus, as did his family. (The phrase in verse 52 is used elsewhere in Scripture to indicate this sort of saving belief in Jesus.)

So, evidently, there are layers of belief. We believe, but we can come to believe even more. The official believed Jesus *could* heal his son. He then came to believe He *would* heal his son. And finally he grew to believe *in* Jesus. This is, of course, one of the aims of pilgrimage: to deepen the beliefs we hold.

This is why we have to face certain fundamental questions over and over again throughout our lifetime. At each encounter our understanding of the issue deepens. For example, this has been my experience with the whole question of evil. While in college one of my close friends was stricken to the very core of his faith by the question of evil. He could not understand how an all-good, all-loving God could allow evil to exist. It was a period of real crisis for him. At the time, I hardly understood what the issues were. But out of all this I did learn one thing: there is a real problem in fitting together the nature of God with the fact of evil. This was not a problem that bothered me at the time. I suspected, however, that one day it would. Sure enough. Years later, after seeing a film that was incredibly violent (one of the early spaghetti Westerns), I was struck by the depths of the problem. How could wanton killing of innocent victims be reconciled with a loving Father? At the time I can remember thinking that if there was any answer to this age-old issue, it must be found in Christianity. After all, Jesus had come and endured evil in His own being. The answer to evil, it seemed to me, had to be found in the person and work of Jesus. I think at the time I even started writing a sermon on this theme.

More time elapsed. The next phase in my thinking about the question of evil came as a result of attending a week-long seminar conducted by a well-known Christian teacher. It soon became evident that he viewed God as a rather stern authority figure, who was quite capable of inflicting all manner of punishment on disobedient mankind! This conflicted sharply with my own understanding of God as a loving Father. Which was right? This started a chain of inquiry which is not yet complete. Out of this, however, I have come to see in a new way the complexity of the issue of evil. I am not quite as certain now of some of my views as I once was. I have a great deal of work to do in this area.

In other words, it is seldom adequate to say of a concept, particularly a fundamental one, "Oh, I believe that" and leave it there. Rather, our understanding and our belief ought to grow and deepen over the years, as we faithfully follow the pilgrim way.

But what if this questioning leads us to disbelieve what we once held to be true? In fact, this will happen. Again the problem is not so much with the nature of truth as it is with our flawed understanding of it. As a new Christian we tend to "believe it all." If an older Christian says that something is so, we accept his word without hesitation. If you ask a young Christian to draw up a statement of faith, it would go on for pages and pages, containing not only an affirmation of his belief in Jesus as his

Savior, but his belief in the need for abstinence by Christians and his trust in the Pauline authorship of Ephesians. You name it, he believes it. But as our pilgrimage goes on, we come to realize the vast difference in importance between believing Jesus to have risen from the dead and believing in the Pauline authorship of Ephesians. Our faith becomes more and more focused on the really important issues, while secondary beliefs become of less practical significance, and certain beliefs drop away all together, as we discover that they are not biblical but cultural in orientation. One of the results of pilgrimage is the honing down of our faith to the real issues, and then the deepening of our belief at these points.

We come back to our original problem: how do we distinguish between questioning which leads to disbelief and that which results in growth? By now it should be evident that there is no straight-forward, unambiguous answer that can be given. Faith, doubt, questioning, disbelief are all intertwined. When it comes right down to it, a great deal depends upon our attitude. If we really want to grow, we will. Our questions, our doubts, even our disbelief will all merge to produce growth. If, however, we are comfortable with the *status quo,* if we really do not want to change our views, if we are not open to new input, then these same factors can be used to justify our lack of movement.

The temptation is to argue that since doubt can lead to disbelief, the counsel of prudence is to so insulate believers that they will not come into contact with doubt-producing ideas. But it is virtually impossible to isolate a person so totally that he will not come into contact with the prevailing, anti-Christian belief of the culture around him. Heaven knows, it has been tried. Certain groups of believers have invested a great deal of time, energy, and money into constructing a self-contained world complete with Christian schools (nursery to university); Christian businesses and Christian social life; buttressed by a local church whose activities consume most of one's spare time; whose teaching creates a distrust of all outside influences; and whose sanctions are severe enough to deter all but the intrepid. Yet still, young people grow up and leave the faith.

Why? For one thing, given this era of radio, T.V., and other mass communication media, as well as the complexity of an economic system which necessitates interdependence if a business is to survive, it is impossible to prevent individuals from coming in contact with prevailing cultural values.

And when people, particularly young people, do come in contact with such ideas, the meeting is often devastating. For the past several years, a friend of mine has been working in a job that brings him in contact with students at a leading Christian college. He has had the chance to speak to literally hundreds of these students over the two years. And, he told me, it has been exceedingly rare to find any graduates who have survived very well after they left the college. Everything was great while they were a part of the tightly-controlled college environment, surrounded by those of like persuasion, confident in their shared convictions. But once the students left and had to cope with the real world, their lives began to fall apart. He gave one example. The divorce rate, he estimated, was nearly 30%—one out of three marriages of these students broke up, many within a few years after graduation.

How much better if these students could have been prepared for their encounter with the secular world by examining together in the context of the Christian college community the anti-Christian ideas, values, and attitudes that proved so devastating. Then they would not have been so intimidated the first time they met someone who argued persuasively, for example, that God could not possibly exist, or that Christian sexual morality was archaic. Without the ability to think for themselves, and without prior exposure to threatening ideas, Christian young people will continue to leave their faith when they come across the first hint of dissent.

There is one other thing that we can do to lessen the chances that hostile ideas will overwhelm a person and lead him away from his faith. We can seek to create the sort of climate in which it is possible for there to be an on-going *experience* of the reality of God. I have a good friend who grew up a hard-boiled empiricist. He believed in only what could be measured. One day he was sitting in a church. This in itself was extraordinary but he had felt that his children were reaching the age where some "moral training" would be useful. So he had gone to the nearest church to see what it was like. This is how he came to be sitting through a special "Youth Service." He wanted to know first-hand what his kids would be receiving there. Quite unexpectedly, in the middle of this service, he had one of the mystical experiences I described in Chapter 7. He was overwhelmed by the presence of God. Later he told me that this was the only possible way for him to have come to faith in God. He could never have been argued into the Kingdom. His ideas were too fixed. But this *experience* had by-passed all his intellectual defenses (which were formidable; he is a university professor with a Ph.D in science). In the end, it is experience, not thought, that overcomes doubt.

The issues surrounding doubt, faith, questioning and unbelief are not simple. We do doubt. We cannot help doing so. Yet this doubt can be the stepping stone to new convictions. Or it can lead us away from Christianity. The difference often lies in our attitude (do we want to believe or is skepticism more attractive to us); in the environment in which we exist as Christians (are we part of a community in which there are the intellectual and personal resources to help us in confronting some of these thorny questions); and in the nature of our experience (do we cultivate our inner life in such a way that we grow in our experience of God). The pilgrim must walk a difficult path between doubt which overwhelms, and isolation and avoidance which stagnates. It is this narrow path, however, that leads to wholeness.

Lack of Motivation

If fighting our fears is one task we must undertake, finding motivation is another. If there is one problem that is more common than any other for the person who has been a Christian for years, it is the loss of motivation. We look back with a certain nostalgia on the beginning of our Christian life when we did everything with enthusiasm and gusto. We dreamed grand dreams then, freely gave of our time, energy and money to every Christian project, and spent vast amounts of time at church. This is no longer true. We are still active in the church perhaps, but without great enthusiasm. We still support certain Christian projects but our giving is much more calculated. In short, our Christian life has lost a lot of the dynamism we once knew. It is not nearly so much fun now.

This worries a great many people. Their commitment to Christianity is deep and authentic. Their lives have been conformed in many ways to Christ's teaching, and their hope is in the Gospel. But something is missing, and they would desperately like to recover what is gone. What happened along the way to quell this ardor? The answer is quite simple: we have lost our sense of direction. When we become a Christian we find a new direction for our lives. We are overwhelmed by the discovery that we can walk in God's way and so find fulfillment for our aspiration to be whole and know the truth. But this discovery does not remain fresh and invigorating forever. In time, despite the fact that we could never imagine losing any zeal, our Christian life becomes routine.

Many things conspire to dampen our enthusiasm: disillusionment with other Christians (whom we once saw as the epitome of spirituality); bad experiences in Christian organizations (the same ones that once meant so much); the sheer routine of our Christian involvement; disappointed expectations (we prayed, but nothing happened); circumstances; plans frustrated through stupidity or blindness—there are a lot of reasons.

No matter what the specific cause, it seems to me that ultimately the result is a loss of direction. We are no longer quite sure what God wants of us. We have lost touch with that unique purpose which is ours. We may not even be all that far off the mark, but nevertheless the result is that we come to wonder why we are doing what we do. Without a sense of meaning, we flounder. There is no big secret as to what we must do to reignite our inner dynamism: we have to recover a sense of purpose. We have to recapture the awareness we once had that we are doing what God has called us to do.

This is easy to point out. It is not so easy to do. Yet there are several things that can be said. The first step is to become aware that we have lost touch with God's direction for our life. What we do then will depend upon who we are. We may seek out our pastor and discuss the whole problem with him. Or we might start reading a book about how God leads His people. We may revert to the ancient practice of fasting as a means of clarifying our perceptions. In any case, the crucial thing is that we begin to listen with care and attention for God's voice. We seek His word to us in our circumstances, through the words of others, and in the inner depths of our personality. When we begin to listen, we can be sure that in the fullness of time, we will hear. It may not be immediately. It may not be with the word we expect or in the manner we anticipate, but we will hear. And in hearing, we are renewed: we rediscover our purpose. We get back on target. We start moving again with purpose and with new enthusiasm.

Five years ago, my family and I returned to the United States and I began work with a new Christian communications company. When we accepted the new job both my wife and I had the sense that this was where God wanted us. Yet we both also sensed that this new job would not be permanent. Sure enough, after two years of struggling, the company had exhausted its limited production resources. Some useful materials had been produced, but revenue from these was insufficient to launch any new projects. We met as a company and decided that we could no longer continue in this fashion.

Since this turn of events was not unexpected, my wife and I anticipated that we would quickly move on to the new thing God had in store for us. I had several interesting prospects. But a quick move was not in God's plan. In fact, in the year to follow, while I considered a host of new possibilities, I never felt the freedom to accept any of these jobs.

As the months passed, my frustration grew. Why wasn't God opening up the new thing? I began sleeping poorly. I worried about how I was going to pay the bills given the fact that I had only a temporary job (despite the fact that both Christian organizations I had worked with had suffered recurring financial problems and yet we had never wanted).

Quite unexpectedly one night, I had a dream. As the details began to unfold, I grew aware that this was no ordinary dream. There was important information in this dream, information that related to the direction I should be pursuing in my life. The specific details of the images are unimportant. The fact was that I clearly saw what I should do.

I woke up with a great sense of excitement as soon as the dream finished. I knew what my next step should be and the implications of this raced through my mind as I struggled unsuccessfully to get back to sleep.

This was not at all the way in which I expected God to speak to me. My whole background was contrary to the notion that God any longer used such means. And yet His voice was unmistakable. I knew what I must do. From that point onward I began to experience a new and unexpected sense of motion. As I threw myself into the new task, I found I did so with a gusto I had forgotten I had. And as I applied myself, it was with a deep sense of satisfaction.

In the time since that experience there has been a new and deepening sense that I am indeed walking in the way I ought to be. In fact, it is clear now that even the months of waiting had a real purpose. The new path is not what I had anticipated. Certain turns in it were quite unexpected. For example, I still have the "temporary" job I took when the communications company floundered. But it is a path that has come to make real sense; and in fact, possibilities I never imagined have opened up.

Loss of motivation is not all that uncommon. There is so much in this modern life that is capable of distracting us from the direction in which we must go in order to be faithful to God's purpose and to find wholeness in our life. Hence, it is necessary for the pilgrim constantly to be alert to the possibility that he is straying from his course. Once he is aware that this has happened, it is then a matter of seeking a new sense of direction. Once sought, direction will come and the journey goes on.

▶ Inter Action

Fighting Fears and Finding Motivation

There are two distinct parts to this exercise. The first deals with fears, the second with motivation. Undertake whichever exercise relates to where you are as a person. Whatever you decide, read over both the exercises since they contain approaches which might one day be of use to you.

I. Fighting Fears

A. What sorts of things are people afraid of? Make a list of as many fears as you can think of.

(Example: snakes, death, other people, loss of job, being wrong, kids getting hurt)

B. Now circle those fears which you share.

C. Look at each of these personal fears. How can they inhibit your growth or limit your freedom?

(Example: Loss of Job—limits one to "secure" position so one never steps out and thus test his skills in new areas)

D. In what areas have these fears affected your life?

(Example: fear of kids getting hurt—am overprotective, don't let kids go it alone enough, too pre-occupied with their safety)

E. Group together all these fears which are "fear of what might happen." One by one, consider how probable each fear is, and what you can do to prevent it from occurring. You might also consider the roots of such a fear (*e.g.,* you fear losing your job because your father once lost his job and you had an awful time). In what ways can you prevent each fear from having a detrimental effect upon your life? (*e.g.,* you have got to realize that people lose jobs all the time, and that you will cope if you do, and henceforth, you must take more risks as far as your career is concerned). Note also those possibilities over which you have little control (*e.g.,* death) and consider how you must learn to live with such eventualities.

F. Now look at the rest of the fears. These will probably relate to real problems you are having right now (*e.g.*, the fear of people will influence countless decisions). These are fears which you really ought to seek help in overcoming. They will, in all likelihood, be serious detriments to your growth. However, identification of them (which is the point of this exercise) is the first and often biggest step in overcoming them.

II. Finding Motivation

To get back in touch with God's purpose for our life is essential in order to recover the dynamism in our Christian experience. However, as I pointed out in the previous chapter, it is not possible to outline any infallible method for coming to know God's mind. God is God, and He speaks as He chooses. Yet we can prepare ourselves to hear His voice. Often our problem is that we have stopped listening. We have grown insensitive to His voice.

The following is an exercise in listening to God. Unlike the previous exercises it cannot be completed in a day. Rather it is an outline of various steps which can be taken over a period of time in order to grow more sensitive to God's voice.

A. Set aside a section in your Growth Notebook for this exercise.

B. The first portion of the exercise is a study in remembering. It will provide the foundation upon which the rest of the exercise will rest. Its aim is to help us locate where we are now in terms of understanding and aligning ourselves with our purpose in life. This will take a half hour or longer to complete, so do not begin it until you have at your disposal a block of uninterrupted time.

1. Begin by sitting in silence for a few moments with your eyes closed. Let your breathing become slower and more relaxed. In this situation, open yourself to the question of where you are now in your life. Don't try to construct this answer consciously. Just inwardly feel the shape of your present life. What characterizes your life now? Who are the key people? What are your main concerns? Where is your time and energy directed? What groups define this period? What concepts or ideas are most important? As various images and feelings come to you, jot them down, without losing your inner concentration.

Now ask yourself: What is my purpose during this period of my life? What image comes to mind as you open yourself to this question of purpose? Try to hold this image in your mind. Open yourself to it. Let it develop. All the time jot down brief notes to describe how this image is forming, just enough so that you will recall all this later on. Slowly open your eyes now.

Read back over your notes. Jot down further thoughts and feelings that come to you as you do this. Now you have a base from which to work, a sense of where you are at this moment in time in reference to the overall purpose of your life.

2. The next step in this process can be undertaken now or later. This consists of noting those turning points in your life that led you to where you are now. Make a list of those incidents, events, experiences, decisions, that have shaped your direction. For example, your choice to go to college would be a turning point. How did you come to that decision? What happened to you subsequently, in terms of purpose, as a result of this decision? List eight or ten such turning points (You might want to go back to your pilgrimage charts as you try to recall turning points.) Sometimes these will be distinct events: "I was driving from Boston to New Haven, thinking about the struggles of the past year to know what to do when I graduate, when all at once it became very clear that I was supposed to go to graduate school and not to take any of the jobs I have been offered." At other times, our life shifts direction as a result of a whole series of events in one period of time—so it is the period, not a single event, which is the turning point.

Scan this list of turning points. What do these say about your progress in life? How do your past decisions correlate with where you are now? How does the past harmonize with the present? Are there discontinuities?

3. What of the future? Is this present period drawing to a close? Just beginning? What are the future possibilities that are opening up to you? Note as best you can the options of which you are aware that are now open to you.

At this point, engage in some fantasizing. First, have you fulfilled past leadings? If you sense that you may not have done so, that there are aspects of your calling which are incomplete, fantasize various ways you could respond to these. For example, at one point you may have sensed a strong pull toward writing, but certain decisions led you away from that option. In the here and now, how could you act on that desire? Your list could include such possibilities as: enroll in a creative writing course; try to get a job at a publishing house; spend each lunch hour writing short stories; go off to Tahiti and concentrate on writing. Remember, this is fantasizing. Don't let the sense of what is possible or realistic enter into your thoughts.

Second, what do your desires at this moment tell you? If you could start over, right now, what would you really like to do? Again, fantasize. Don't let "realistic considerations" enter into your calculations.

C. The preceeding work was by way of preparation. It was an opportunity to get in touch with your past and dream about your future. For the Christian pilgrim, however, it is not enough to sit back and calculate, based on past experiences and future possibilities, which way to go. He really wants to know God's mind in all this. This is not to say that the past has no significance nor that future intimations are without meaning. It is just that what one wants is the sense that we are indeed proceeding on the basis of call and not merely launching out on the basis of our best human calculations.

It is time, therefore, to take what we have learned and sensed, and seek to know God's mind in all of this. The following is a list of possible ways we can go about seeking that Word. Use whatever approaches make sense to you. In all this, remember, what we are really doing is opening ourselves to God. We cannot dictate nor even ever anticipate how or when He will lead. We simply trust that He will.

1. There are a fair number of books about finding God's will. It can be very useful to work through one of these like Elisabeth Elliot's *A Slow and Certain Light: Some Thoughts on the Guidance of God* (Word Books, 1973), or *Guidance,* by Oliver Barclay (Inter-Varsity Press).

2. You will want to pray about this matter of direction. In fact, this is the time to learn about prayer as dialogue (if you have not already discovered this). Prayer is not just a matter of non-stop speaking on our part. It also involves learning to listen for God's voice in the stillness (as I discussed in Chapter 8). Books like *Have Time and Be Free,* by Theodore Bovet, *How to Pray,* by E. Stanley Jones, or *Creative Prayer* by E. Herman can be studied with profit—if they are used as springboards to prayer on our part and not merely as the means by which we learn more ideas about prayer. It is in the silence of prayer that we grow conscious of God and hear His voice.

3. It is often difficult to find adequate time in the midst of our busy existence for such quiet contemplation. Perhaps we need to take off a day or two and go on a retreat. Such times alone, especially if connected with fasting (which apart from anything else produces moments of amazing inner clarity), serve to put us back in touch with ourselves, with God, and with our purpose in life.

4. Such periods of time provide the opportunity for inner dialogues of the sort I discussed in the Inter Action section of Chapter 6. Using as background the insights you gained in Step B of this exercise (this is the time to read over this material again), hold inner dialogues with your present circumstances, with your job or career, with your desires and ambitions for the future, and with your "purpose in life." Out of these dialogues, some of the "dreaming" you did may emerge as the very thing you ought to pursue.

Be alert also for what your dreams may be telling you. Dreams are an expression of the inner images which comprise the world of the unconscious. As such they provide a means of coming in touch with the indigenous world of our unconscious which is both mysterious and powerful. Dream-language, however, is symbolic in nature, and hence we must learn to understand it (as will be discussed in Chapter 12), so we must beware of jumping to conclusions based solely on dreams.

5. So far I have been focusing exclusively on an inner search for direction. However, this is not to say that other people have no input for us. Often, in fact, other people see much more clearly the problems facing us and the opportunities we should explore. It is very useful to talk over our situation with friends or relatives, or with our pastor or even a professional counselor.

6. In all this a certain perserverance and patience are needed. We will hear what we need to hear if we stay open long enough. In the meantime, the process of becoming sensitive to circumstances and other people; of searching out new insights via study, prayer and inner dialogue; of turning our attention to the supernatural, is the very stuff out of which new growth emerges.

7. There is one more thing that must be said lest what I have written lead to misunderstanding. The Christian walk is not a matter of waiting until we hear a specific word from God before we dare take a step—like the woman in Joe Bayly's story who prayed about whether she should put her new African violet on the left or the right side of the bookcase.[1] We don't always know exactly what to do. We walk by faith not by sight. All we need to know is that we are walking in obedience to the sight we do have. My concern in this section has been with the problem of getting in touch with the central direction our life should be taking—our loss of zeal being a fairly reliable (though not infallible) sign that we have lost sight of this.

Part IV
Resources for Growth

As the world must be redeemed in
a few men to begin with, so the
soul is redeemed in a few of its
thoughts and works and ways to
begin with: it takes a long time
to finish the new creation of this
redemption.

—George MacDonald

11 External Resources

As should be abundantly evident by now, pilgrimage involves ongoing learning. It is when we gain new insights into the way things are and begin to adjust our lives in accordance with what we have found, that we grow. This being so, an obvious problem is: Are there resources available that promote such learning; and if so, how do we best take advantage of these?

The answer to the first part of the question is obvious — one need only glance at a Christian periodical to discover the number of growth resources that are being offered to the American public. In fact, this sort of browsing can be a jolting experience as I discovered when—acting on my own advice—I leafed through a magazine that was on my desk. I found there a dizzying number of items being hawked—ranging from new Bible translations (one of these was a translation of the Bible into the language of motion pictures) to extension courses in theology. There were a bewildering number of books mentioned, an announcement of a new Christian film and a forthcoming Christian T.V. special, as well as the offer of cassette tapes of outstanding Christian speakers. One intriguing ad included a coupon which could be mailed in if a person wanted to become a dealer in personal growth resource material—helping others, as it were, while earning extra money. The only thing missing, it seems, was an ad I had seen in previous issues for a Christian vacation tour to some exotic place lead by a famous Christian speaker.

Looking through this magazine was a depressing experience in many ways. Some of the material was probably quite good. A lot of it, however, seemed to be second-rate, and I kept wondering if the main reason it was offered was financial. After all, merchandising to the Christian market is big business these days. In several cases, the particular resource could be utilized only by the rich. If you were poor, well, you would have to be content with something else. I suppose the most troubling aspect of all this was the implicit assumption that seemed to pervade the magazine: "If you have problems in your Christian life, here is just what you need to set things right." There was almost a medicine-show atmosphere to some of the ads with their offer of quick remedies to complex problems.

The one bright spot was the fact that there really are a lot more growth resources available now than ever before. I can recall the difficulty I had in finding adequate materials for use in follow-up programs that I set up some years ago. There were only a handful of Bible studies available then, precious little small-group resource materials, and almost no media material (apart from a few films). Of what was available, most was not suitable content-wise for new Christians, nor was it particularly good from an educational viewpoint. We have come a long way in a short time, it seems, in producing an abundance of resources.

The second part of my question—how do we best take advantage of these growth resources—provides the reason for writing the rest of this chapter. It is evident from the sheer abundance of material that we have to be discriminating in our use of these resources. We have to learn the strengths and weaknesses of each type of resource as well as become aware of how we individually learn best. Then we can perhaps find some of this material useful without being overwhelmed by all of the available choices.

For me, I suppose, books have been the prime resource I have used throughout my Christian life. I love reading, always have, and so it was natural that I would turn in this direction in my Christian life. Books, however, are not without problems. For one thing, we cannot assume (as some seem to do) that merely by reading something in a book this insight will become a part of our lives. Growth is not that simple. It is true that what we read may spark a chain of events that eventually does influence our life-style, but finding the insight in a book is only the first step, not the last. Secondly, not all books are of equal value, nor, for that matter, can we trust everything we read in a book. This is obvious when it is said, but in fact many people tend to treat books as if they were almost sacred. Yet a great many books published each year are not worth the paper on which they are printed. Likewise, a lot of things which find their way into print are simply not true. For books to be useful to us we have to develop a sense of discrimination. We have to learn not to waste our time on certain books and we have to develop the ability to spot faulty arguments or misleading statements in those that we do choose to read.

In this regard, one of the more useful books I read while in seminary was Mortimer J. Adler's *How To Read A Book*. Adler's aim was to outline the rules for coming to grips with a book. It was his contention that there is an *art* to reading a book and this must be mastered before a person can begin to maximize the usefulness of literature. Adler ends his book with an interesting observation. He suggests that it is far more important to read the relatively few great books than to tackle vast quantities of other books. In other words, the most significant learning comes from in-depth encounters with a few truly excellent books, rather than from quick reading of a number of mediocre volumes. This is a valuable caution as we face the sheer volume of books available to us.

It is probably important to point out that growth-producing literature does not necessarily have to be written from a Christian point of view. Insights that produce growth are not the exclusive property of Christians. In recent years, my own pilgrimage has been helped enormously by the writings of Carl Jung and certain of his disciples (*e.g.*, Ira Progoff), who, while not anti-Christian, do not write from an exclusively Christian position. The hesitation of some Christians to expose themselves to "non-Christian books" is an off-shoot of that fear described in the previous chapter—the fear of doubt. When we limit ourselves in this way we greatly reduce our potential for growth.

The other side of the coin is that not everything written by a Christian author (no matter how distinguished) is necessarily true. All authors— Christian or not—suffer from the same handicap: no one is able to see or know everything clearly. So it is not enough to read only those books written by well-known Christians and published by "sound" Christian publishers, and assume therefore that what we read is true. Whether the author or the publisher is Christian or non-Christian, we are still faced with the need to be discriminating. I suppose it is the high regard Christians in general have for the Bible that leads some of them to blindly trust certain authors and publishers, just because they happen to be labelled "Christian."

Most of us, it seems, are haphazard readers, *i.e.*, we pick up a book that captures our fancy, read it, and then move on to another, unrelated book. There is little planning in our study. This is not necessarily bad. In fact, such random reading means that we are exposed to a wide variety of subjects and this is enriching. However, at times we will want to focus our reading in a specific direction because we have a concrete problem. For example, we come to see that our lack of meditation is a hindrance to our growth. So we turn to books like *A Testament of Devotion* by the Quaker scholar Thomas R. Kelly or *A Serious Call to a Devout and Holy Life* by William Law that can be of help to us in developing a meditational life. These in turn might lead to books that deal with specific aspects of meditation—like prayer (and we read *Prayer* by O. Hallesby) or Bible Study (and we work through *Creative Bible Study* by Lawrence Richards). In other words, we may need to shift from random reading— out of which we gain insight into our need to tackle specific areas—to directed reading.

At other times it is refreshing to study a particular author rather than a single subject, or just books in general. In this way we can come to grips with the growth, struggles, and insights of one person. A man like C. S. Lewis, for example, is a delight to study. He writes so well and in such a wide range of fields that one does not tire of him quickly. With Lewis, you could begin with his classic *Mere Christianity,* then read his book on prayer, *Letters to Malcolm,* before moving on to one of his essays like *The Abolition of Man* or *Miracles.* At the same time, you could be reading his delightful children's books, *The Chronicles of Narnia.* When you finish all these, you would still have ahead Lewis' novels, his apologetics, his poems, his sermons and short essays, his letters and his biography as well as his autobiography. By following such a course, one eventually comes to feel that Lewis is not just a distant author but a personal friend who has shared with us a host of incredible insights. We also come to know and understand his particular world-view—with all its idiosyncracies and color, and we are enriched by the experience.

All this is not to say that the Christian pilgrim reads only 'serious' books. In fact, in my own reading, I consume a fair amount of fiction, especially (these days) science-fiction. And I have found, not surprisingly, that there are all sorts of valuable insights that emerge out of this 'fun' reading. Essays and other weighty literature do not have the corner on truth. Also I have found that I need this lighter reading to balance the other material. Otherwise, it is all too easy to get bogged down in a 'serious but important' book that requires great energy to get through.

We are still left with the problem of choosing, out of all the possibilities, those books worth reading. The surest way to find good books, it seems, is to develop the art of reading. When we learn how to interact with books, then we can usually tell whether we want to read a particular book simply by spending a little time going through it. One way of getting leads on good books is by asking friends about the two or three significant books they have read during the past year. It is also useful to glance at book reviews—or talk to the owner of your local bookstore (if that person is a bibliophile, that is, and not just a merchandiser). I have also found that one good book leads to another. If I am excited about a particular book, there is a fair chance that I will also be excited by the books which the author recommends.

Despite all I have been saying, it is obvious that books are not useful to everyone. For one reason or another, certain people do not read much. There is no great shame to this. It is simply a fact that different people learn in different ways. It has been said that President Kennedy was a voracious reader but that his successor, President Johnson, learned best through conversation with informed individuals. The style of learning is not important. That we do learn is the essential thing for the pilgrim.

Like President Johnson, many of us learn best by means of direct interaction with other people. In fact, this is a rich but often overlooked means of learning. All of us are surrounded by scores of people, each with a different background, with different experiences, and with different insights—in other words, with the sorts of people from whom we can learn. In the give and take of discussion we are exposed to new ideas and perspectives, which we have the opportunity to question and examine then and there. Unlike the experience of reading in which all we have to go on is what is set down in type, in dialogue we can probe behind the ideas until we really understand them. This same probing is also directed at *our* ideas—which forces us to clarify our thoughts. A person who exposes himself to on-going dialogue is not allowed the luxury of half-understood ideas or unthought-out beliefs—and this in itself is vital to our growth. Also, as we enter into the give and take of sharing, we find ourselves becoming more concerned, more loving human beings—and this is the essence of pilgrimage. But conversation, like reading, is an art which must be learned. It involves learning how to share our ideas and learning how to listen to the ideas of others. It is not as easy as one might think to speak about those things that really concern us. It takes a conscious decision on our part to be open and honest. The temptation is to hide behind the safety of bland subjects. Yet in so doing, we introduce an element of dishonesty into our relationships. To speak about our garden when in fact we are desperately concerned about the future of our job (or deeply interested in a subject like healing), is to deny ourselves the chance for new insights into these areas as well as to deny our friends the opportunity of coming to know us.

But just as we can slowly learn to read more perceptively, so, too, we can learn to open up more in dialogue. This will involve learning to crystalize our own thoughts and concerns—so that we can speak about them coherently. We will also have to develop the willingness to share these concerns with others. We will have to learn to listen, too. All too often we merely 'hear' the words of another person (while our real attention is on what we plan to say in response or even on a completely different subject), whereas in active listening, our full attention is focused on what that other person is trying to say to us. Active listening is the key to real learning in dialogue. Not only do we thus open ourselves to the insights of another, but active listening also serves to draw out that other person. "Here is someone who is really interested in what I have to share," he feels, and so opens up more and more.

So far I have focused on the process of informal learning, i.e., drawing out the insights of friends and acquaintances. There is also a more formalized way in which we learn from other people: we can attend lectures, seminars, classes and sermons in which a person gives a structured presentation of an idea or concept. This is a traditional and valuable means of learning. As with books, the quantity and quality of lectures seems to have grown in recent years. Lest anyone doubt this all he needs to do is to examine the bulletin board of any college and behold the array of lectures advertised there. The average church has its fair share of speakers (not to mention a minimum of 52 sermons scheduled each year). In fact, in even a medium-size city, it is quite possible to attend a seemingly endless round of lectures if we so choose. On top of all this, with the advent of audio and video cassettes, it is now possible to listen to the world's best speakers in one's living room.

In addition, there are more adult education courses being offered than ever before. With the student population declining, colleges are offering extension courses that are open to everyone, thus providing an unparalleled opportunity for discovering and developing new skills, for opening up whole new areas of understanding, and even for developing new careers. It is possible to study specific subjects—ranging from the academic (*e.g.,* "Archeology and the Bible") to the practical (*e.g.,* "Pottery Making") and including many growth-shaping opportunities (*e.g.,* a course on Values-Clarification). It is safe to say that almost any subject can be growth-producing if it meets a need in us and thus gives a new balance to our lives or pushes us to explore unfulfilled longings.

There is one further type of personal interaction which must be mentioned. I refer to a counseling relationship with another person. In this instance we seek out a professionally trained person (or perhaps just a very wise, compassionate friend) in order to discuss (and hopefully overcome) a specific problem in our life. There are some problems, it seems, that simply will not go away without such help—and they remain as blockages to our growth until dealt with.

Such help is more readily available now than ever before. Apart from anything else, seminaries are offering more and better courses in counseling so that today's minister is often well equipped to diagnose and treat problems. Ministers have also learned to spot severe problems that go beyond their training and will in such cases refer an individual to a qualified specialist. Gone are the days when couselling consisted of good advice and a couple of Bible verses.

It must be added, however, that there still does remain a certain hesitation among some Christians when it comes to seeking counseling. There is a fear that a therapist will undermine one's faith. This fear has some basis to it. At the beginning such psychology was anti-Christian. Certainly Freud saw religion as a problem to be overcome, and behaviorism has never really had a place in its scheme for religious experiences. But, today, in more than one psychological framework, the religious experience is understood to be both real and healthy and there are scores of counselors who are themselves Christians. This is not to say that no psychologist will ever seek to undermine a person's faith or morals. It is to assert, rather, that good counseling is available; and often, it is the pastor who will be in touch with such therapists, and can make referrals.

Small groups are another formalized means of conversation. A group of people gather in a home for an evening, but rather than engaging in the usual chit-chat, they turn their minds to a particular topic. Perhaps they study the prophecies of Jeremiah or discuss problems in marriage. They may be meeting together to talk about a book which everyone has read or they may use a kit of small group materials to guide their interaction. Whatever the agenda, the aim is similar—the group of people are seeking to grow in some way by means of the special type of interaction which is possible in a small group.

It is this 'special type of interaction' that makes small groups unique. Something happens when not more than twelve or thirteen people gather to discuss a particular topic in a setting that allows for face-to-face interaction. There is a give and take, a sharing, a mutual support that can be quite overwhelming. One does not simply learn new ideas in a small group, one is supported and loved in the life situation that requires the learning of these new things. In a small group that is functioning properly, there is warmth, acceptance, honest sharing, forgiveness and mutual encouragement—hence an atmosphere highly conducive to growth and change. This is not to say that all small groups unfailingly exhibit such positive characteristics. They do not. Small groups can be dull, tedious, and sometimes even destructive. But on the other hand, time and time again the special magic of love is there and the overall experience is reviving.

Despite their great value, small groups have not always been popular within the church. While it is true that small groups have cropped up at various points in church history (*e.g.,* Wesley organized his converts into groups of twelve), this has been the exception, not the rule. It seems that whenever there has been a strong emphasis on ecclesiastical authority, small groups have been unpopular. During such periods, the ordinary Christian was expected to listen and obey, not to interact and discover, as one does in a small group. Today, however, small groups are very popular in the church, due in part to the recent research by social scientists into the dynamics of small groups, which has demonstrated just how effective small groups can be in promoting change in an individual's life. The church has not been slow in taking advantage of these findings and using this tool in its programs. As a result, there are excellent small group resources available. To mention just a few, there is Keith Miller and Bruce Larson's course, *The Edge of Adventure;* "New Options for Christian Community Through Base Church Groups," by Charles Olsen; and the Serendipity Books by Lyman Coleman. The latter is a series of really engaging interactive exercises written for all different age groups. Certain groups like the Institute of Church Renewal in Atlanta and the Creative Resources Division of Word Publishers are committed to publishing a wide variety of such resources.

The availability of such resources means that almost anyone, with some training and a certain amount of prior small group experience, can run an effective group. Hence it is possible for a few like-minded people to get together informally and begin their own study group, investigating issues which are of concern to them and vital for their personal growth. No longer is it necessary to wait until the church (or some other body) decides to sponsor a seminar on "Creative Parenthood," for example. It is not all that difficult for a few concerned parents to put together their own study group—using the abundant materials on this subject (books, articles, kits, cassettes, etc.) and cashing in as well on the special dynamic a small group offers.

Lyman Coleman, who wrote the Serendipity course, has taken his small group materials a step further than most. Each year he offers seminars all over the country on how to use these resources. However, what is ostensibly a seminar on small group techniques turns out to be as well an experience in growth itself. By means of the Serendipity material, Coleman is able to guide a small group of strangers from the point of first meeting one another through to the experience of real warmth, communication and caring by the end of the day.

This is illustrative of yet another type of resource—the retreat or conference during which a person leaves his normal environment for a day or longer and concentrates his attention on a particular subject. Retreats and conferences are not new, of course. Who hasn't been to a high school camp? But today what is new is the sheer number of such opportunities, the wide range of topics treated, and the sophistication of the educational resources used. No longer is it simply a matter of twenty or so young married couples from the church spending the weekend together at a conference center with the pastor of a nearby church speaking five or six times. Now, hundreds (or even thousands) of people gather at a convention center in some major city and listen to speakers from around the world, participate in carefully planned interactive exercises, and engage in specialized workshops. This is not to say that the older, less sophisticated retreats are *passe*. The fact that they are closely tied to a person's on-going, daily life (all the people at the retreat are friends) means that they deal with issues directly related to all those attending. This immediacy often outweighs the brilliance of the lectures one might hear at the larger but more annonymous conference. In any case, the fact remains that real growth results from those special times when we go away for the purpose of an in-depth look at some area of our life—whether we go to a huge conference, to a retreat center with a few friends, or simply go off on our own for a day's meditation.

So far I have been discussing opportunities for *receiving* the sort of input that leads to growth. Often, however, growth comes when we seek to *give* to others in one way or another. This is, of course, learning by doing—a time-honored method of education as well as a vital aspect of our whole Christian calling. God gives to each of us special gifts with the intention that we use these for the sake of others. Such gifts lie dormant or shrivel away if unused.

Today there are countless opportunities for Christian service—even (or especially) in the local church. There one can teach Sunday School, lead a youth group, serve on one of the administrative boards, run a small group, etc. There are also any number of inter-church, or independent ministries that need help—like Young Life, or "Christians for Urban

Justice" (an inner-city ministry in Boston)—not to mention all the worthy causes that are not church connected but deal with basic human needs. In whatever way a person gets involved, he will be called upon to exercise his gifts and skills. A Sunday School teacher, for example, if he is really concerned about communication, will find all sorts of areas in which to develop his skills. He may, for example, investigate educational techniques in order to improve the effectiveness of his teaching. Or he may research media resources which can serve as an adjunct to his weekly presentation. Certainly he will want to investigate in detail the subject he is teaching. Such learning, since it has a specific goal, usually takes place at a greater depth than when pursued merely for the sake of learning itself.

In fact, creative projects of any sort—whether they are goal-oriented or merely expressions of some sort of inner vision—are almost always growth-producing. To write an article, lead a Bible study group, tutor children with reading problems, capture a personality in oil paint, organize a rally to protest urban injustice, all require us to search out new data as well as to draw upon inner talents. It is not that one simply decides, "I think I'll do something creative today." Rather, it is when these activities are done in response to our understanding of our calling that they make sense and produce growth.

It is possible to go on listing resources for growth. I have not discussed, for example, the way films and T.V. can stimulate growth, nor have I touched upon such unusual endeavors as communal living as a stimulus to growth. My aim, however, is not to produce an exhaustive list of resources. After all, when a person has been a Christian for a while, he is well aware of all these external resources. These are part and parcel of American Christianity. In fact, our blind reliance on such outside input to produce growth for us is often the reason why we have stopped growing—but this is the subject of the next chapter. In any case, our problem will not be that we can't find any external input that promotes our growth. Our problem will be in deciding what input we must *reject* in order to focus on the one or two that are vital to us. The temptation will be to undertake too much—or even more likely, to think that since we are so busy we must be growing. Yet it is not enough to read six books, hear five lectures, belong to four groups, subscribe to three magazines, attend two conferences, and teach Sunday School—and thus conclude that we are making progress. We may be, but then again, all this may be merely random activity—full of much effort but unrelated to what we need to be about in order to fulfill our purpose in life. Such undirected activity is often self-defeating. We are busy as Christians but still we have no sense that the activity means anything. Running in circles is very exhausting after awhile. The real question is whether we are utilizing those resources which can serve to help us become all we can be. How we choose what is right for us is the subject of the Inter Action section.

▶ Inter Action

Using Resources

We are surrounded, even overwhelmed by growth-producing opportunities. The question is, how do we choose from among all these options just what fits our needs? Before we get to that question, however, there is a prior consideration: is there *time* in our busy schedule to fit in any new activity? In other words, can we make room in our life for all these marvellous opportunities?

I. The Time Problem

In *Have Time and Be Free,* Theodore Bovet mentions a test whereby we can gain some insight into the way we use our time.[1] He suggests that you:

A. Make a list of the principle interests that go to make up a person's life, such as family, friends, vacation, athletics, art, study, religion, meditation, social affairs, sleeping, eating, etc.

B. Write after each category a number between one and ten, to indicate the value that you place on each interest.

C. Then in a second column, enter the amount of time you spend during an average week involved with each item. (The total ought to work out to 168 hours!) To do this you will probably have to spell out your time table on an average weekday and on an average weekend.

D. Now examine the discrepancies between what you say you value and how in fact you use your time. Few of us will find a perfect correlation between our use of time and our priorities. Are there any really glaring discrepancies? What can you do about them?

E. The real question is how to open up your schedule in a way that will enable you to find time for growth and involvement without neglecting other priorities. This may involve cutting down on the amount of time you spend sleeping or playing baseball (both quite legitimate activities). It may mean giving up old commitments for the sake of new ventures. Each case will be different. To complete this exercise, look again at your list. What interests are occupying too much time? Too little time? In what ways could you free up hours to be diverted to an adult-education course, for example? Are there old commitments which can be given up? How could your limited time be used more creatively?

II. Which Avenue?

To know which direction to go will depend on several factors.

A. Summarize how you understand the nature of your calling as a person. This is the issue you dealt with in Chapter 10.

B. Now go back over your pilgrimage charts and try to identify the ways in which you best learn. How did growth take place in the past?

C. What is the growing edge in your life, *i.e.,* at what points do you sense the need to grow; what are the unresolved issues which are facing you right now; where are the tension spots in your present experience?

D. What really interests you at this point in your life? What could you get excited about?

E. Look over your response to these four questions and see if you can isolate either a question to which you need an answer or an area in which you must grow.

F. In each of the five areas I have discussed, list what you know of the possibilities that exist that bear upon your particular concern. Try to be as specific as possible. You may have to do a little research. What courses are being offered in your area? Are any conferences planned? Where can you get advice about the best books to read?

G. Scan this list and choose one or two approaches that feel right to you.

H. Now make concrete plans in terms of your schedule to undertake what you decide upon.

12   Inner Resources

So far, most of the resources I have discussed are familiar. There may be a wider selection of books than ever before, more sophisticated conferences, and better-run small groups. But nonetheless, this is familiar territory. Traditionally we have turned to such outside stimuli to gain insight and direction in our Christian life.

It has not always been so. In New Testament times, not many people read and those who did had few written materials from which to choose. Nor were there any trained pastoral counselors, multi-media kits for use in small groups, or extension courses in theology. Yet still, the people grew in wisdom and knowledge. To be sure there was preaching, teaching, and abundant opportunities for service. But there was also something else. And it is this 'something else' that I want to discuss in this chapter.

In a word, what made all the difference for the first century Christians was their *inward sense of being in touch with the living God*. Christians grew not so much because of their use of external resources, but because they knew God within and listened to His Voice. They grew because they nourished this inward way of knowing. Throughout the New Testament writings, one finds this sense that the essence of the Christian experience was that of being intimately in touch with the Living God. John writes: "We know that the Son of God has come and given us understanding to know who is real; *indeed we are in him who is real, since we are in his Son Jesus Christ*" (I John 5:20). Paul declares that the task assigned to him by God is to announce "the secret hidden for long ages. . . . The secret is this: *Christ in you* . . ." (Col. 1:25-27). Jesus Himself says: "I am the Vine and you are the branches. He who dwells in me, as I dwell in him, bears much fruit" (John 15:5). Over and over again it is stated that the Christian is "in Christ," or that Christ is in him, and I am convinced that when the New Testament authors spoke this way it was not merely a turn of phrase used to indicate that someone was a follower of Jesus. They meant exactly what they said. The essence of Christianity was some sort of inner communion or inner experience.

As science developed, western man turned his back on inward realities. More and more people concluded that we live in a closed universe in which all is "determined." What was real was now thought to be that which could be felt or seen or heard. To mention love (or any emotion for that matter) was to speak of certain physiological responses. To consider man more than a mere cipher in an unfathomably vast universe was arrogance. To imagine that mankind had been made in the image of God was pious nonsense. The church itself was not immune to such perceptions. More than one theologian sought to construct a non-supernatural theology. Dreams, prayer, God's guidance, miracles, visions, healing—the very currency of the New Testament experience—was quietly forgotten. The western Christian began to look outward for the meaning and essence of his faith.

This perspective is now in the process of changing. In the last thirty or forty years, science has done an about-face (largely on the basis of the findings of theoretical physics) and has begun to concede the possibility of an open universe. In addition, disillusionment with technology has opened our culture to the inward ways of the East, with the result that there is a growing awareness that there may be more to reality than mere sensory impressions convey. The anti-supernaturalism of many of the traditional churches has begun to disappear under the influence of such things as the charismatic movement with its emphasis on experiential Christianity.

This revolution comes none too soon. More than one commentator has noted the growing barrenness within modern man. While outwardly mastering an incredible technology, inwardly he is lost. This loss of meaning "is a matter of emotional emptiness and eventually of *ennui* and psychological disturbance. It is expressed in physical ailments, in the search for artificial pleasures, and, more fundamentally, in a feeling of boredom and cynicism that hovers in the background of all personal relationships. It hollows out life, and it has become one of the major problems of modern industrial culture."[1]

Ironically, it is western science that has opened the way to this new awareness of the nature of inner reality. At the turn of the century, Sigmund Freud in his rigid adherence to scientific principles succeeded in demonstrating clinically that such a thing as an unconscious exists, *i.e.,* he showed that there is an inner realm of reality common to all men which is independent, largely unknown, and yet capable of influencing our conscious experience. The revolution in understanding the nature of our world had begun.

At about the same time that Freud was demonstrating the existence of the unconscious, William James, the famous American philosopher and psychologist, was delivering the Gifford Lectures on Natural Religion at the University of Edinburgh. He entitled this series "The Varieties of

Religious Experience: A Study in Human Nature." James was among the first of the psychologists to address the question of religious experience and he did so both perceptively and sympathetically. Apart from anything else he took his informants seriously when they told him that they had been transformed from "a former divided self into a unified self" (to use James' words) as a result of coming into contact with "something beyond themselves." In trying to summarize what happens to various individuals during such transformational encounters, James concludes that when "the stage of salvation arrives, the man identifies his real being with the germinal higher part of himself; and does so in the following way. *He becomes conscious that this higher part is conterminous and continuous with a MORE of the same quality, which is operative in the universe outside of him, and which he can keep in working touch with. . . ."*[2]

The nature of this MORE intrigued James. Was this really "God" that men experienced and did they do so via the unconscious? A few pages later he writes: "Let me then propose, as an hypothesis, that whatever it may be on its *farther* side, the 'more' with which in religious experience we feel ourselves connected is on its *hither* side the subconscious continuation of our conscious life. . . . The theologians' contention that the religious man is moved by an external power is vindicated for it is one of the peculiarities of invasions from the subconscious region to take on objective appearances. . . ."[3] In other words, it would seem that it is via the unconscious that man comes to experience God.

This is an exciting insight and one that answered for me a long-standing problem. Even as a new Christian I wondered what it really meant when we talked about "having Jesus in our hearts," or said that "Jesus was a friend closer than a brother." As Christians we urged people to "invite Jesus into their lives" and then pointed out that successful Christian living came as a result of a "daily walk with God." In all these ways we affirmed our belief in an intimate, personal relationship with God. But how could this be? God was not accessible to our senses. We could not see Him or hear Him or touch Him and yet we talked as if we could.

The funny thing was that though I wondered about all this, I never really questioned whether Christians were simply putting people on with all this talk about knowing God. The reason was that I had had myself certain experiences in which I was aware of the power and presence of God. For example, late one Sunday evening while in college, I felt a strange compulsion to pick up my Bible and read it. I had never had such a sensation before. Even as I picked up my Bible I *knew* that somehow this would be a significant experience for me. I didn't have any idea what I was supposed to read so I simply opened the Bible at random. (I never did that sort of thing. I thought it was superstitious nonsense to pluck random verses like magic from the Bible and consider this God's leading.) The chapter to which I turned was Matthew 28. I began reading at verse 16, and as I did so it was like nothing I had experienced before.

The verses were no longer written words to me. They were spoken—and they were deeply personal and directed specifically at me. At that moment there was no question in my mind that this was God speaking to me. As I read verse 17, I could not understand how it was that some of the disciples doubted when they saw the resurrected Jesus on the mountain. How could they, I felt, my whole being throbbing with the awareness of God's presence. But it was verse 19 that most caught my attention. "Go therefore and make disciples of all nations." This was not simply a command to the original apostles. This was God's word to me and it was spoken to me. "Lo I am with you always." This was His personal benediction.

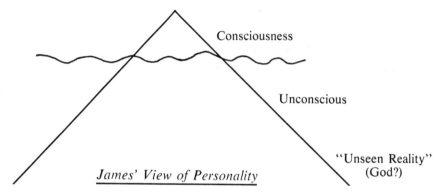

Consciousness

Unconscious

"Unseen Reality"
(God?)

James' View of Personality

That experience not only shaped the direction my life took, it was also the sort of encounter that made it impossible for me to doubt that men could experience God. My problem was not: "Could this actually be?" but: "How did such encounters take place?" What was the nature and dynamic that made possible this divine-human interaction? It was in reading William James that I first began to understand. James arrived at his views about how man is able to experience God because of his understanding of the nature of human personality. James, it seemed, envisioned human personality almost like an iceberg. The tip of the iceberg, the part that shows above the water, is our consciousness—the seat of awareness, the focal point of our senses, the home of our thought and feeling. Just below the surface is what James called the "subconscious." This is the "hither side" of the *more*—"the subconscious continuation of our conscious life." Deep down in the dark waters is the *farther* side of the unconscious, touching, so it would seem, another Reality—God, if the theologians are right (though James will not commit himself unequivocally). To my mind, the important point that James makes is that it is the unconscious ("subconscious" is his word) that provides the link between man's personality and God's nature. It is in the very depths, at the root of our personality, that God speaks.

This concept explained for me how it is possible for man to know God. It explained the "still, small voice;" the intimations of leading from God that we "feel;" the "mysterious raptures" that mystics write about and the way in which dreams (the voice of the unconscious) are used by God to speak to us.

In 1917, Rudolf Otto published his now-famous work, *The Idea of the Holy*. He, too, was concerned about the nature of religious experience. His inquiry took the form of an analysis of the experience of the Holy. He begins by noting the universal "feeling-response" of awe, fascination, and even dread in the face of that which the person considers holy. He calls this feeling *mysterium tremendum*. It is characterized by the sense of having confronted the Wholly Other, toward whom we feel not only awe and dread arising out of a sense of the absolute unapproachability and overpoweringness of the Other, but also fascination, so that we long for and seek after the *numinous* (his word for that which meets us in such experiences). He cites example after example of numinous encounters, until he makes his point: human beings have an inherent ability that enables them to know the numinous and this ability is in a special category by itself. All of this fits in nicely with the conclusions of James.

This early work was clarified and developed, however, by the research of Carl Jung. From the time he published his doctoral dissertation in 1902 until his death in 1961, Jung wrestled with the problem of the nature of man's religious experiences. The outcome of his research was a theory of personality in which religious experience is seen as shaping a central part in our growth and development. In many ways, Jung's theory of personality is simply an extension of James' basic hypothesis with more of the details filled in. Jung, like James (and others), begins with the idea that man's nature consists of two parts—the conscious and the unconscious. The unconscious, Jung says, has three layers. First there is the *personal unconscious*—which is that part of our personality that is just below consciousness and not difficult to gain access to (James' 'subconscious'). We all know the experience of 'forgetting' something, only later to recall it again. Likewise everyone has experienced a 'slip of the tongue' ("Where did that come from," we wonder). These forgotten or repressed experiences make up the content of the personal unconscious.

However, Jung pointed out in one of his greatest discoveries that the unconscious is not merely the repository of forgotten events and repressed experiences. There is an even deeper stratum to our personality—and he called this the *collective unconscious*. Unlike the personal unconscious, which is individual in nature (*i.e.,* its contents are a direct reflection of the experiences of a particular person and it is therefore unique for each man), the collective unconscious is similar in nature for each and every person, regardless of culture, period of history, or ethnic background. In other words, the contents of the collective unconscious are universal in nature. Jung called these contents *archetypes*. He detected their existence by the observation that the same motifs he found in his patients' dreams, fantasies, deliria, and delusions were also found throughout the world's literature, both ancient and modern, especially in myths and fairy tales. Ancient Greek myth-makers were captivated by the same images that arise out of the unconscious of modern man.

The third and deepest layer of the unconscious is the so-called 'psychoid reality' from whence the archetypal images arise. This portion of the unconscious is virtually inaccessible. Little is known about it. Its existence, however, is derived from the fact of archetypal images. It is the reality which lies behind these images. Furthermore, it seems to be polar in nature—involving on the one hand instinctual drives and on the other spiritual realities. The word "psychoid" itself means 'something more than just psychic.' Jung's 'psychoid reality' sounds suspiciously like James' MORE—that is, a reality which touches our unconscious on one side and spiritual reality on the other. Putting this all together into a sketch, the human personality as understood by Jung would look something like this:

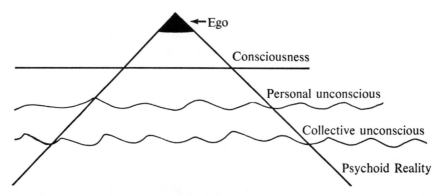

Jung made another startling assertion. He said that the ego was merely the center of our *conscious* life, not the core of our personality. The real center of our being is the Self—which is the central archetype found in the collective unconscious. Furthermore, he said that in coming to experience this archetype of self we experience God, *i.e.,* we have the impression of coming into contact with that which is 'Wholly Other' (to use Otto's phrase)—and that out of this encounter we find wholeness. In other words, religious experience is not just an embarrassing lapse brought on by a temporary unbalance in our psyche, as some would say. Such experiences are vital to our very growth as people.

Since archetypes play such a central, albeit mysterious, role in our life, it is important to look a bit more closely at their nature. Technically speaking, archetypes are "primordial images," "universal tendencies of behavior," "self-portraits of the instincts," or "psychic processes transformed into images" as they have been described by various people. Experientially, we come to know archetypes through various images that make themselves known in our dreams and reverie. Among the more common images are those of the "Great Mother," the "wandering hero," "paradise," and the "wise old man." Each of these images opens up new insights into our nature as we come to recognize and experience them. Central to all the images, however, is the Self. The Self is the center point of man's being. It is that which defines who we really are and gives shape to our life. It is the Self that guides the unfolding of our personality. It is the Self which provides for us a picture of wholeness. As Jung writes: "Empirically it can be established, with a sufficient degree of probability, that there is in the unconscious an archetype of wholeness which manifests itself spontaneously in dreams, etc., and a tendency, independent of the conscious will, to relate other archetypes to this center. Consequently, it does not seem improbable that the archetype occupies as such a central position which approximates it to the God-image. The similarity is further borne out by the peculiar fact that the archetype produces a symbolism which has always characterized and expressed the Deity. . . . The God-image does not coincide with the unconscious as such, but with a special content of it, namely the archetype of the Self."[4]

In other words, the Self which is the center of our being, which is a symbol of the wholeness we seek, this same Self is also an image of Deity. It is God's stamp on our personality. It is what biblical writers would call "the image of God" in man.

This is a breath-taking concept. By purely empirical means Jung has arrived at the same conclusion as to the nature of man's personality as have biblical writers. Both would say that there is written right into the core of personality the image of God, and it is this image which is a symbol for us of the wholeness we seek as pilgrims. The implications of this are clear. To become whole it is necessary to come in touch with this center. It is vital to open ourselves up to our inner world. Growth is not merely a matter of reading books and attending meetings. It involves a coming in touch with our inner nature and learning to grow and move in response to what we find on this inward quest. And we do this when we start to pay attention to the images that make up the dreams and visions that arise in the course of meditation or in the process of active imagination, and that stimulate and compel the creative energies in us.

All this may sound strange to our western ears. Yet what I have just said would not sound at all strange to the ear of a Christian living in the first century. For him, the fact that God spoke through dreams, sent visions, and met man inwardly was assumed. This assumption is written all over the Bible. On virtually the first page of the New Testament a dream is mentioned. In Matthew 1:20 an angel tells Joseph in a dream that Mary will bear a son conceived by the Holy Spirit. In Matthew 2:12, the wise men are warned in a dream not to return to Herod. In Matthew 2:13, Joseph is told in a dream to flee to Egypt. In Matthew 2:19, he is told in another dream to return to Israel because Herod has died. In Acts 9:10, Paul's great vision is described, out of which came his conversion. In Acts 10:3, Cornelius has a vision that he is to send for Peter; who himself is having a vision which was to change the very nature of the church (Acts 10:17ff). The Book of Revelation is a product of visions. And so it goes on. How ironic that it has taken modern psychology to call our attention back to the original experience of Christianity!

It is not too surprising that the road to wholeness seems to lead straight to the inner world of experience. For many people, it was an inner experience that caused them to become Christians in the first place and it was the awareness of this new, inner reality that provided the dynamic for their early Christian life. But time intervenes, and the memory of such encounters fades. This in itself is not bad. We cannot go on living on the basis of one experience. The problem, however, is that we have not been taught to go on exploring this inner world of the spirit that has been opened up to us. It is almost as if the Church says: "That sort of experience is dangerous stuff. One encounter with God is enough. Now you will have to be content with getting on with His work in the world." There is, of course, an element of truth to this. We are meant to get on with the work of the Gospel in this world and some people find this inner world so fascinating that they lose effective touch with the reality around them. But this perception misses the mark, too. What we really need is balance, *i.e.,* an on-going, sustaining sense of God's presence which provides for us the dynamic and direction necessary to do His work in this world.

If this is the case and the key to on-going growth lies within us, the remaining question is: How do we open ourselves to this inner world? The answer is simple. We begin to pay attention to our dreams, start to utilize techniques of active imagination and other meditation aids, and seek to open ourselves to God in our silence and prayer. It is, of course, far easier to point this out than it is to begin to practice it. In my own life, I feel that I know far more about the unconscious than I experience. I feel like such a novice in the face of the enormity of the world within. It is so difficult to overcome our outward orientation. But, like so many other steps along the way in our pilgrimage, once we are open to a new insight, all we need do is to take the first small step in that direction. This will lead to a second step and so we find ourselves on the way, albeit slowly, with much hesitation, and not without a certain looking back.

The most natural place to begin the exploration of the inner world is with our dreams. Dreams are the language of the unconscious. However, it is not always easy to get in touch with our dreams. Although everyone dreams, there seems to be real differences among people when it comes to remembering dreams. Yet most people can learn to recall dreams. What it takes is, first and foremost, a real desire to remember our dreams. The next step is to have a pencil and paper right beside our bed. Dreams are clearest during the first few moments after we awake—so it is vital to put them down on paper as soon as possible. Fifteen or twenty minutes after we wake up is usually too late.

Once we have a dream down on paper, the question is: What does it mean? It is obvious that dreams are not *logical* in nature, *i.e.,* they do not follow an orderly sequence with the intention of making a specific conceptual point. A dream is not like a book. Rather, a dream is *symbolic* in nature. It consists of images that move and flow and unfold. Hence, it is necessary to learn the language of dreams in order to discover how to interact with their rich and strange symbolism. However, dream interpretation is a large subject in itself—indeed the subject of a book on its own. In fact, I would suggest two books that can profitably be consulted as the next step in learning to understand dreams. These are: *God, Dreams and Revelation,* by Morton T. Kelsey and *Dreams: God's Forgotten Language,* by John Sanford, both of which are written by Episcopal ministers. However, at the risk of oversimplifying the subject, let me make a few suggestions as to how we can come to understand our dreams. The first step is simply to start collecting dreams faithfully, so as to acquaint ourselves with this new landscape. As we do so, we will begin to note recurring figures and symbols. It is these recurring images that we can use to begin our work of interpretation. When you spot one of these key symbols, perhaps due to its recurrence in your dreams or perhaps simply because it is so magnetic that it dominates a dream and draws attention to itself—focus your attention on it. What thoughts spring to mind? What does this image suggest to you? What importance might it have? Could it symbolize any part of yourself in any way (often the figures in dreams are symbols for aspects of our personality)? Write all these musings down in your journal. Next let your imagination take hold of the symbol. Perhaps you might want to try to express in clay or by a painting what this symbol means to you. In any case, let it grow and develop in your imagination.

Out of this process, in due time, clarity and insight will come. Be forewarned, however—a dream is not like a scientific discourse which has only one meaning to it. There is no absolute meaning to a given dream. Different people will interpret the same dream in different ways. Even when we ourselves come back to a dream (or symbol) at a later date we will probably see new elements in it. But this is the nature of a symbol—it suggests various meanings and is not exhausted by a single look. In fact, it is really only over a period of time that the intent of our dreams becomes clear—as we let the imagery develop night after night, unfolding its meaning to us (and, if Jung is right, correcting any wrong interpretive tracks we might be taking).

If at all possible, it is valuable to discuss your dreams with another person. Best of all, of course, would be a person experienced in understanding dreams. The guidance of such a person is the easiest and best way to grow familiar with the language of dreams. However, discussing dreams with someone close to you has real value. Often the other person will be able to suggest meanings we overlook (perhaps they are uncomfortable to us). At other times, the sheer act of sharing our dream with another person will suggest meanings to us.

Learning to understand our dreams will take time. After all, what we are doing is learning a new language. But gradually, as we gain experience and grow familiar with our inner world, so, too, we will develop the sort of intuition that leads us quickly to the intent of our dreams.

As I hope is evident, one of the really important factors in dream interpretation is the use of our imagination. It is this imaginative facility that unlocks the meaning of the symbols. In fact, our imagination itself provides a second way into our inner world. There are different ways to use our imagination. We can carry on inner dialogues as I have already discussed. Or, we can let our inner imagery make itself known via a fantasy which we let happen, without controlling it. Or, we can use any one of a number of meditative techniques. Whatever course we choose, the intent is the same—to tap into the ever-flowing, ever-present swirl of images that make up our inner world. For it is in that world that we find the guide posts that direct us toward meaning; it is there we are warned of dangerous tendencies in our life; it is there that we begin to see ourselves in new and honest ways; and it is there, especially, that we meet God. It is He, after all, whose Reality and Presence meets us in the depths of our unconscious, at the center of our personality.

My intention in this chapter has been merely to point out the reality of the inner world and its relationship to our growth; and to suggest (without detail) ways to come in touch with this world. Obviously the next step will require additional input. In this regard, let me make two suggestions. First, there are two books that will repay study. Morton Kelsey's book, *Encounter With God: A Theology of Christian Experience* (Bethany Fellowship, Inc.), seeks to set Christian experience into a framework of history and theology. He describes how men can and do experience God. The final section of his book is practical in nature, outlining what he considers the twelve rules for coming into contact with the inner world of experience. Tolbert McCarroll's book, *Exploring The Inner World* (The Julian Press, Inc.), is, as its sub-title suggests, "A guide book for personal growth and renewal." In it McCarroll discusses such things as dreams, art experiences, meditation, using a journal, and inner imagery. McCarroll's book provides a fine overview of the various ways to explore our inner selves.

My second suggestion is to attend, if at all possible, a workshop, seminar, or conference that seeks to help people open up to this inner world. I remember the enormous help I received by attending a Dialogue House workshop one weekend a year ago. Dialogue House was founded by Ira Progoff, the Jungian-trained therapist whose books I have referred to several times already. Progoff's aim over the years has been to develop a means whereby individuals can make contact with their interior life and grow to know themselves at an even deeper level—*largely as a result of their own efforts*. In this way, he has opened up many of the insights of psychoanalytic psychology to more people than just the few who can afford the time and money to enter into an orthodox patient-therapist relationship. Progoff calls his approach the intensive journal method, and outlines it well in his book *At A Journal Workshop: The Basic Text and Guide for Using the Intensive Journal*. Progoff's journal workshops are given at locations around the country and a schedule can be obtained by writing Dialogue House at 80 East Eleventh Street, New York, New York, 10003, or by calling, toll-free, 1-800-221-5844.

The path toward wholeness has many twists and turns to it. Eventually, however, we have to return to the root of our Christian experience, *i.e.,* to the world within ourselves wherein we meet and know God. Perhaps as much as anything, the willingness to journey within marks out the pilgrim. The settler is often such because of the fear he has of what he might find within. So he attempts to tame and to institutionalize the Christian life. He substitutes dogma and formulas for experience and seeks thereby to make a safe Christianity. God, of course, keeps breaking out of whatever boxes we construct for Him and so men and women go on experiencing Him in all His Otherness.

There is a valid impulse, however, behind our desire to flee from such raw, unfiltered experience. Such subjectivity can and does go awry (as do many other good things). Dreams are taken too literally and weird behavior results. Men meet God and conclude that thereafter when they speak, it is God's word they utter. Individuals discover that others pay attention to them when they claim to have revelatory experiences and they grow to enjoy this power (sometimes even faking expeiences when the real ones disappear). Subjectivity does have dangers to it. But then, so does objectivity. Witness the sterility of so many totally orthodox people who know and believe every doctrine. Yet despite the danger, the way back to the joyous, motivating experience we knew when we first became Christians is via this inward path. The Christian really is *in Christ* and Christ is *in him*. And to grow we must learn to open ourselves to this inward Christ so that we are renewed and empowered for the work to which he calls us in His world.

▶ Inter Action

Inner Visions

In doing the suggested exercises, you have already begun to get in touch with your inner life. The attempt to become aware of the way you felt about the image of the pilgrim, for example, was an exercise in understanding a symbol. Likewise, the inner dialogue you undertook in chapter six was an experience of active imagination. Both this process of symbol clarification and that of active imagination are powerful tools that you can continue using in your inward journey. The following exercises focus on three additional tools.

I. A Journal

On this journey of self-exploration you will need a journal in which to record your progress and findings. You have, of course, already begun this. Now it is time to expand your original pilgrimage notebook. You should add at least two new sections—one in which to record your dreams and your work with them, and a second which you might entitle "Active Imagination," in which to record your fantasies and other musings of the imagination.

Using a journal successfully requires a certain amount of discipline. We must set aside time to use it regularly. The ideal would be to log our dreams each morning as we awake and then to log what happened during the day before we retire—recording the impressions, insights, and experiences that made up our experiences for that day. In addition, we should take time to interact with the symbols of our life—via doodling, active imagination, fantasy, or inner dialogue. The ideal is not easy to obtain and perhaps we have to be content at first to use our journal every three or four days. The important thing is to begin and to keep going, as regularly as possible.

Using a journal is also an art. I know of no more complete discussion of journal-keeping than Progoff's *At A Journal Workshop* (Dialogue House Library). Study of this book will pay rich dividends even if one is never able to attend an Intensive Journal Workshop.

Essential to all journal-keeping is honesty. We may not like all we see and hear but still we must record it. In fact, it is this inner honesty which makes a journal so important to growth. All of us have areas of inadequacy, points of self-deception, and ugly flaws in our personality. Likewise, none of us enjoy facing these parts of ourselves. But if we are honest in our journal, these negative sides will emerge and can therefore be dealt with. It is as necessary for our growth that we confront the shadow in us as it is that we discover signposts that give us direction.

II. Meditation

This inner journey is no new thing. Mystics down through the ages have been walking in this way, and in so doing have developed a variety of exercises that can aid us along the way. In addition, in recent days due to research into bio-feedback, brain wave patterns, and other related subjects, whole new methods of meditation have been developed. The following books will be of use to you in exploring meditation:

A. Ira Progoff has done a new translation of one of the classic guides to spiritual experience: *The Cloud of Unknowing* (A Delta Book, 1957).

B. *The Imitation of Christ* by Thomas à Kempis is another classic work which has been of substantial value to countless individuals.

C. *Mysticism* by Evelyn Underhill and *Mysticism: Its Meaning and Message* by Georgia Harkness will introduce you to a wide variety of mystical writers as well as help you to understand the strange and wonderful world of the mystic.

D. Chapter Six in McCarroll's book *Exploring the Inner World* deals with meditation.

E. As well as contributing useful insights into prayer, W. E. Sangster and Leslie Davison have also written a chapter entitled "Spiritual Exercises" in *The Pattern of Prayer* (London: The Epworth Press, 1962).

III. Dreams

There is no better time than now to start recording and interacting with your dreams. Outlined within the chapter itself are those techniques you need in order to begin, as well as references to books which will help you on the way.

13   The Dynamics of Change

In 1943, Kurt Lewin wrote what has since become a classic paper, in which he outlined a model to describe how successful change takes place, either on an individual or group level. Lewin said that successful change has three steps:

1. An unfreezing of the present situation.
2. Movement to a new position.
3. Refreezing at this new position.

Since that time this "force-field" model has become widely known and used. The reason for the popularity of this particular model is not hard to discover. Not only is it simple, readily usable in a wide variety of circumstances, but it works. It really does describe what happens to an individual when he undergoes change in his life. As such, it is a powerful tool in the hands of those who seek to instigate change (*e.g.*, social activists, church leaders). It can also be a useful tool in the life of an individual who seeks to grow and wants to understand the forces at work in his life that either promote or inhibit meaningful change.

The first step in "force-field analysis" is to identify and describe the forces that converge in a person's life at the point which is under consideration. According to Lewin, certain of these forces drive an individual toward change while others—*with equal and opposite force*—restrain him from change. It is this balance of forces that results in the quasi-equilibrium of a given position. Change takes place when either the restraining forces weaken or the driving forces increase. So the task of the change agent (be he the individual himself or an outside person) is to work toward weakening the resisting forces or strengthening the driving forces. Change is most likely to take place when both these actions take place simultaneously. When such an imbalance is created, the individual then moves to a new position where once again the driving and restraining forces are balanced and new equilibrium is established.

Let me give an example of what this means in practical terms. Suppose a church is faced with the question of whether to move to the suburbs or stay on in the center of the city. This situation could be described in terms of those forces which favor moving and those which favor staying. Among the driving forces there might be:

1. The deteriorating state of the church building.
2. The relocation of many members to the suburbs.
3. The lack of adequate transportation from the suburbs into the city on Sundays.
4. The racial feelings of the largely white congregation.
5. The increased crime and vandalism in the inner city.

The forces which act to restrain such a move might include:

1. The high cost of relocation.
2. A sense of responsibility to the needs of the inner city.
3. A sense of the history and tradition of the church.
4. The abundance of churches in the suburbs compared to the inner city.
5. The opportunity for facing and working through racial prejudice afforded in the present location.

Various factors could unbalance this equilibrium and precipitate a decision in either direction. For example, suppose the church is offered a high price for their downtown property while at the same time vandalism increases in the neighborhood. This decrease of one restraining force (the high cost of relocation is off-set by the substantial offer for the property) and increase of one driving force (vandalism) could combine to percipitate a decision to move. However, given different changes in the opposing forces, the opposite reaction is possible. Perhaps the minister begins to preach about the need for Christians to overcome their racial prejudice while at the same time developing new and exciting programs which involve the church in the neighborhood. This could serve to strengthen the restraining forces. If this were combined with the offer of assistance from the denomination to repair the building (thus reducing one of the driving forces), the decision could well be made to stay.

It is obvious that Lewin's model gives the change-agent a useful tool for assessing a situation and then for knowing what steps to take to bring about change. It is important to note, however, that it does not tell him in what direction this change should take place. Force-field analysis gives no insight into whether it would be better for the church to stay or move. This is an issue which must be decided in other ways.

So, too, in our personal livesLewin's model can be of immense use to us in understanding the forces that impinge upon us and in knowing how to promote change in one direction or another. But we must look within to find the direction for that change. Should we stay in our present job or move into a new field? Force-field analysis will help us understand which forces tell us to stay and which tell us to move—but whether we *should* stay or move is something to be decided on the basis of how we have come to understand God's will in this matter.

Once again we come back to the need to plumb our inner depths in order to continue on our pilgrimage. Yet this is not unexpected. Jesus told the disciples that it was necessary for Him to go away, to leave them—but that He would send another in His place. This Other was the Holy Spirit who came, not in the flesh as Jesus had done, but into the hearts and minds of those who followed Jesus. His power and presence were every bit as real as that of Jesus—one need only read the Book of Acts to learn that. He spoke, however, in a different way. He spoke within. And so it is within we must turn to discover and to go on discovering what it is that God would have us be and do in this world.

In the end, we must discover by ourselves who and what God intends us to be. When we know this, then our understanding of the dynamics of personal change becomes really useful.

Let me add one final word. In order to draw out the meaning of the two images, I have distinguished quite sharply between the pilgrim and the settler. In real life, that distinction is not quite so rigid. In fact, there are both tendencies in each of us. At times we all behave like true-blue settlers; while at other times, we relentlessly pursue growth. This is the way it has to be, I suppose. Very few people can cope with continuous, unrelenting growth (certainly I, for one, cannot). We all need to balance off periods of change with times of continuity and rest. In fact, it would seem that such times of settling are necessary in order to assimilate what we have been learning. The mistake, as I have tried to point out, is to stop and never move on again.

It is important to know that there is a bit of the settler in each of us. Apart from anything else, this ought to make us more tolerant of others as well as of ourselves. It is probably true that we do not always "press on" to fulfill—or even to find—our calling. But criticism and feelings of inadequacy seldom help us get going. Rather, what all of us need—be we pilgrims or settlers or (which is more likely) a mixture of the two—is love, support, and encouragement. After all, the journey is long. It is not always easy, and there is much to mislead us along the way. It is well to remember the words God spoke to Jacob on his journey through what was to become the Promised Land. Appropriately enough, God spoke to Jacob in a dream: "Behold, I am with you and will keep you wherever you go, and will bring you back to this land; for I will not leave you until I have done that of which I have spoken to you." (Gen. 28:15) This is a promise for all pilgrims to remember.

▶ Inter Action

Plotting Personal Change

As we move on in our pilgrimage we are certain to confront times of real tension. Such uneasiness often signals that we have come up against an area in our lives in which we need to change. Lewin's force-field model provides a powerful tool for helping us to analyze the nature of the problem and then to see what we can do about it.

I. Identify a tension-point in your life (*e.g.*, your feelings toward women).

II. In a paragraph or so, try to define as specifically as possible the nature of the problem (*e.g.*, the fact that the third secretary you have hired this year is now resigning has forced you to realize that you have problems relating to most women).

III. Define the direction in which you want to change in this area (*e.g.*, you want to learn how to understand and relate to women).

IV. Spell out the forces which impel you to change and those which impede change. List these as balancing forces as shown in the example below:

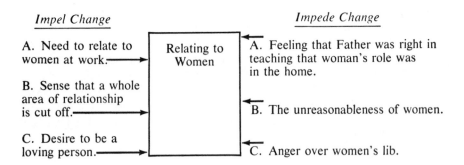

Impel Change		*Impede Change*
A. Need to relate to women at work.	Relating to Women	A. Feeling that Father was right in teaching that woman's role was in the home.
B. Sense that a whole area of relationship is cut off.		B. The unreasonableness of women.
C. Desire to be a loving person.		C. Anger over women's lib.

V. How can you *decrease* the force of those factors which impede change? (*e.g.*, you might join a small group in order to get to know counseling and sort out the messed-up relationship you had with your parents.)

VI. How can you *increase* the force of those factors which impel change? (*e.g.*, you might join a small group in order to get to know women better in the context of love and support which characterizes a small group.)

VIII. What practical and realistic things can you do to implement the type of change you desire? (*e.g.*, you could decide to visit your pastor to discuss the problem with him and get the name of a good counselor.)

Pilgrimage Bibliography

By now it should be clear that it is not desirable to try to pattern our lives on the basis of another person's life. Our pilgrimage is unique. Yet this is not to say that we cannot learn and grow from the struggles and experiences of others. As Evelyn Underhill has put it in discussing the meaning the lives of saints can have for us:

> Their lives disclose to us in all its delicacy and perfection God's creative action in the realm of the soul. As we enter into those transformed and sacrificial lives—some of them so near in time and place to our own—we see what it really means to have one Lord. It means everything else in life subordinated to this one fact: no exceptions. It means Francis Xavier and David Livingstone travelling for Him to the ends of the earth and Father Wainwright living for Him for half a century in one slum; Bunyon going to prison for Him, and Francis de Sales and Fenelon going to Court for Him; Mary Slesser ruling in the jungle and Julian of Norwich hidden in the anchoress cell; Elizabeth Fry facing the criminals in Newgate gaol and Josephine Butler facing the shocked hostility of Victorian piety; Elizabeth Leseur accepting a painful and limited life, Chalres de Foucauld going out into great spaces and dying alone in the desert with His love.[1]

The classic autobiography of pilgrimage is St. Augustine's *Confessions*. C. S. Lewis' *Surprised By Joy* and E. Stanley Jones' *A Song of Ascents* are the autobiographies of two contemporary pilgrims. As for biography, there is Catherine Marshall's story of her husband, *A Man Called Peter*, and Elizabeth Elliot's *Who Shall Ascend? The Life of R. Kenneth Strachan*. The later is unusual for a missionary biography in that it does not portray Strachan as a saint so remote from our struggles that we can learn little. Rather, it is painfully honest and we catch a glimpse of a real man and of how God can use us in the midst of our sense of failure and inadequacy.

John Bunyan's classic, *The Pilgrim's Progress,* is perhaps the best-known book on the theme of pilgrimage. C. S. Lewis has written an updated version which he called *The Pilgrim's Regress*—although he himself confesses, writing in a preface ten years after its original publication, that the book is 'obscure,' focusing as it does on the journey from 'popular realism' to Pantheism and then to Christianity. In Sherwood Wirt's *Passport to Life City,* the pilgrim sets off in a new yellow Mustang. Dr. M. Esther Harding, one of the most prolific Jungians, has interpreted *Pilgrim's Progress* in terms of analytic psychiatry, and in so doing has produced what Jung himself called one of the best studies of Individuation (the Jungian word for the process of confronting the unconscious in an integrative way). The title of her book is *Journey Into Self* (David McKay Co., Inc.). Then, of course, there are *The Hobbit* and *The Lord of the Rings* by J. R. R. Tolkien—stories of pilgrimage told with great power and beauty in the style of a fairy story.

He who would valiant be
　　Let him come hither;
One here will constant be,
　　Come wind, come weather;
There's no discouragement
Shall make him once relent
His first avow'd intent
　　To be a pilgrim.
Whoso beset him round
　　With dismal stories,
Do but themselves confound;
　　His strength the more is.
No lion can him fright;
He'll with a giant fight,
But he will have the right
　　To be a pilgrim.
No goblin nor foul fiend
　　Can daunt his spirit;
He knows he at the end
　　Shall life inherit.
Then, fancies fly away;
He'll fear not what men say;
He'll labour night and day
　　To be a pilgrim.

John Bunyan
1684

Notes

I. Introduction

[1]These are not the only possible biblical metaphors for the Christian life. I chose to use these particular images because they are rich in overtones, because they yield meaningful insights when analyzed, because they are readily understood given our particular cultural setting, and, especially, because over the years they have been useful and meaningful images for me personally.

II. Chapter Two: The Pilgrim

[1]*Civilization in Transition,* CW 10, paragraph 847.

[2]*Ibid.*

[3]*Mysticism* (New York: E. P. Dutton and Company, 1961), pp. 126-127.

[4]C. S. Lewis, *The Last Battle* (London: The Bodley Head, 1961), p. 172.

[5]*Ibid.,* pp. 180-181.

[6]Rudolf Otto, *The Idea of the Holy* (London: Pelican Books, 1959), p. 49.

[7]*A Dynamic Psychology of Religion* (New York: Harper and Row, 1968), p. 160.

[8]William Barclay, *The Letter to the Hebrews* (Edinburgh: The St. Andrews Press, 1955), pp. 167-169.

III. Chapter Three: The Psychology of Growth

[1]"Self-actualization: A Study in Psychological Health," later published as Chapter 12 in *Motivation and Personality* (New York: Harper and Brothers, 1954).

[2]*Motivation and Personality,* p. 202.

[3]*Ibid,* pp. 200-201.

[4]*Toward a Psychology of Being* (New York: Van Nostrand Reinhold Co., 1968), p. 26.

[5]*Ibid.*

[6]*Ibid.*

[7]*Motivation,* p. 116.

[8]*Ibid.,* p. 183.

[9]*Ibid.,* p. 340.

[10]*Ibid.*, 216.

[11]*Ibid.*

[12]*The Death and Rebirth of Psychology* (New York: McGraw Hill Book Co., 1956), p. 262.

IV. Chapter Four: Charting Our Pilgrimage

[1]*The Great Divorce* (New York: The Macmillan Co., 1946), p. 5.

[2]And well it might, in the fullness of time, if Saint Paul is to be taken literally in Ephesians 1:9-10 and Philippians 2:9-11:

> "For he has made known to us in all wisdom and insight the mystery of his will, according to his purpose which he set forth in Christ as a plan for the fulness of time, to unite all things in him, things in heaven and things on earth."
>
> "Therefore God has highly exalted him and bestowed on him the name which is above every name, that at the name of Jesus every knee should bow, in heaven and on earth and under the earth, and every tongue confess that Jesus Christ is Lord, to the glory of God the Father."

[3]*The Horse and His Boy* (London: Geoffrey Bles, 1954), p. 147.

V. Chapter Five: Quest

[1]*Invitation to Pilgrimage* (London: Penguin Books, 1960), p. 18.

[2]Grand Rapids: William B. Eerdmans Publishing Company, 1930, p. 242.

[3]C. G. Jung, *Memories, Dreams, Reflections* (New York: Vintage Books, 1961), pp. 289-297.

VI. Chapter Six: Commitment

[1]*God Our Contemporary* (London: Hodder and Stoughton, 1960), pp. 147-178.

[2]*The Psychology of Christian Experience* (Grand Rapids: Zondervan Publishing House, 1963), p. 36.

[3]*At a Journal Workshop* (New York: Dialogue House Library, 1975), pp. 158-159.

VII. Chapter Seven: Encounter

[1]See also Andrew Greeley's book: *Ecstasy: A Way of Knowing* (Englewood Cliffs, New Jersey: Prentice Hall, Inc., 1974).

[2]From *Autobiography of Dan Young*, ed. W. P. Strickland (New York: 1860, quoted in James, *The Varieties of Religious Experience*, p. 251).

[3]Taken from Chapters 1 and 2 of Finney's *Memoirs* (New York: A. S. Barnes, 1976), quoted in Fern, *The Psychology of Christian Conversion* (Westwood, New Jersey: Fleming H. Revell Co., pp. 68-70).

[4]Quoted by George Jackson in *The Fact of Conversion* (New York: Fleming H. Revell Co., 1908), p. 100.

[5]"The Weight of Glory" in *Transposition and Other Addresses* (London: Geoffrey Bles, 1949), p. 30.

[6]Paul Little, *How To Give Away Your Faith* (Chicago: Inter-Varsity Press, 1966), p. 59.

[7]*Surprised by Joy* (London: Fontana Books, 1955), pp. 178-179.

[8]*Ibid.*, pp. 182-183.

[9]*Basic Christianity* (Grand Rapids: William B. Eerdmans, 1958), p. 131.

VIII. Chapter Eight: Integration

[1]This was first pointed out to me by the Rev. Tom Houston.

[2]See *The Abolition of Man* particularly.

[3]*Have Time and Be Free* (London: S.P.C.K., 1945), pp. 34, 36.

[4]*The Great Divorce*, pp. 5-6.

[5]According to H. R. Mackintosh in *The Christian Experience of Forgiveness* (London: Fontana Books, 1961), p. 201.

IX. Chapter Nine: External Impediments to Christian Growth

[1]*Life Together* (London: SCM Press, Ltd., 1949), p. 15.

[2]*Self-Renewal* (New York: Harper and Row, 1965), p. 9.

[3]It was, of course, Joe Bayly who originated this particular concept of ministry in his humorous (and insightful) book *The Gospel Blimp*.

X. Chapter Ten: Internal Obstacles to Growth

[1]"A Small Happening at Andover" in *I Saw Gooley Fly* (Old Tappan, New Jersey: Fleming H. Revell Co.), p. 40.

XI. Chapter Eleven: External Resources

[1]pp. 12, 13.

XII. Chapter Twelve: Internal Resources

[1]Ira Progoff, *The Symbolic and the Real* (New York: McGraw Hill Book Company, 1963), pp. 8-9.

[2]*The Varieties of Religious Experience* (New York: The Modern Library, 1902), pp. 498-499. The italics are William James'.

[3]*Ibid.*, pp. 502-503.

[4]*Psychology and Religion: West and East*, CW 11, p. 757.

XIII. Chapter Thirteen: The Dynamics of Change

[1]*The School of Charity*, 1934, p. 33.